Step by Step
Discarding

Danny Roth

B.T. Batsford • London

First published 2000

© Danny Roth 2000

ISBN 0 7134 8611 2

A CIP catalogue record for this book is available from the British Library.

Typeset by KEATS, Harrow on the Hill

Printed by Creative Print and Design Wales, Ebbw Vale

for the publishers,
B.T. Batsford, 9 Blenheim Court, Brewery Road
London N7 9NT

A member of the Chrysalis Group plc

A BATSFORD BRIDGE BOOK
Bridge Editor: Phil King

CONTENTS

INTRODUCTION

Having none, partner?

If you cannot follow suit, you have to discard and, notably early in the play, you will, in suit contracts, have the option to ruff or consider a wide choice of other discards. Later on in the proceedings, however, life can become very embarrassing and, at all levels of bridge, mistakes abound. Especially in the pairs' contests, with all the modern ideas about competitive bidding, various kinds of doubles and countless other gadgets, I firmly believe that, with every trick counting significantly, the prizes are won and lost in the area of defence in general and discarding in particular. I have lost count of the number of tops and bottoms that have changed hands through thoughtlessness and carelessness in this department.

There are two basic sources of error. The first, I am afraid, is down to poor teaching. Beginners are taught never to discard from such holdings as: ♠Kx, or ♡Qxx or ◊Jxxx or ♣10xxxx for fear that their honour, left insufficiently protected, will be subsequently swallowed by higher honours. Once they learn these rules, they stick to them religiously (I have lost count of the number of times intermediate and even experienced players have talked to me about 'Old traditions die hard!' and 'You can't teach an old dog new tricks!' and 'XYZ said: '. . .' XYZ being a well-known name) and will continue to throw contracts and overtricks galore at declarers, while being fully armed with their standard excuse. The second is that it is very easy to lose interest when defending with a very poor hand. Most players like to bid and declare, accepting that passing and defending are two of the necessary chores of the game which have to be done but "the sooner they are over, the better".

If you are going to be successful as a defender, your attitude on both counts will have to change dramatically, but it will be well worthwhile. Remember that, unless you are a consistently good card holder (and I am well below the working class in this respect), and/or a very aggressive and/or selfish bidder (again I am at the other end of the scale), you will, on average, defend two hands for every one you declare. So it is well worthwhile putting some effort into your defence. Even forgetting that it is far more satisfying to win with bad cards than with good, it will also pay dividends to have a reputation of being a good defender. Opponents will treat you with a lot more respect and you will tend to be allowed to declare more hands than otherwise.

It is well accepted that defence is the most difficult aspect of bridge, but I have made the point in a previous book and repeat it now that I am not quite so sure. The common argument is that, while both declarer and defender can see twenty-six cards, the declarer has at least two advantages:

Firstly, he knows exactly what his and enemy resources are while the defenders may be ignorant as to which important cards are kicking which way;

Secondly, as he is operating both his own hand and dummy's, he can arrange for the two hands to play in perfect cohesion while, with the defenders, there are two minds at work and, as many partnerships will tell you, they are not always on the same wavelength.

That all sounds sensible, but one very important point has been missed, namely that the defenders very often have more information. The declarer, notably in a high-level contract bid against silent opposition, knows little or nothing apart from the opening lead. The defender, however, has heard at least one bid from declarer and, especially in this modern era of highly sophisticated systems, will often have been given a complete dossier on declarer's shape and point-count. That is not to mention declarer's early play, which will usually be most enlightening. He is, therefore, far better placed to play 'double dummy', effectively seeing all four hands.

For this reason, there is often little excuse for poor discarding and, as we progress through this book, you will learn to take a totally different perspective and, on occasions, why it is right to hold on to the three-two doubleton in one suit while blanking a king in another. A number of basic guidelines will be laid down and you will find that, if you follow them, the number of silly and expensive discards you make will drop through the floor and you will be saved a great deal of post-mortem misery and rebuke.

First of all, what are we trying to achieve? In my previous books, I stressed the importance of the seven roll-calls. They are as follows:

1) The number of spades in each of the two unseen hands.
2) The same for hearts.
3) The same for diamonds.
4) The same for clubs.
5) The same for high-card points.
6) The number of tricks obviously available to, or easily establishable by, declarer.
7) The same for defenders.

It seems a lot of work, but you are helped by guiding limits:

Each player has thirteen cards.
There are thirteen cards of each suit in the pack.
There are forty high-card points in the pack.
Thirteen tricks will be played in all.

Thus you can base your calculations of the seven roll-calls on the basis that your answers must be consistent with the guiding limits laid down in the above paragraph. A few basic examples will illustrate:

a) A player opens a weak two spades, guaranteeing six cards in his suit. Early in the play, he shows out after the first round of hearts and again after the second round of clubs. He is now likely to be 6142, i.e. you can count him for four diamonds.

b) A player opens a weak no-trump (12-14 points); early in the play, he shows two aces and a king. That is eleven points so, if you are wondering about another ace, it will be with your partner.

c) A pair reaches 7NT and dummy goes down with eight obvious top tricks, but only one ace. Early in the play, declarer shows a king. So you now know that declarer has his eight tricks in dummy, three other aces and that king, twelve in all. Thus, if there is any other king outstanding, it must be with partner, otherwise declarer would have claimed his contract long ago, putting you out of your misery.

You see the idea, but it is amazing how few players take the trouble to do these exercises in simple arithmetic at the table and defensive mistakes abound as a result. Even top-class names all too often fall from grace.

Notice one very important point. I have not yet said "discard this; do not discard that," or anything of the kind. The only thing I insist on is that you work the hand out. From the seven roll-calls above, we now have to anticipate how the play is going to proceed and, in particular, how many rounds of each suit are likely to be played. Thus, if it is obvious that four rounds of spades will be played, then, unless you visualise your hand ruffing, it will usually be right to keep four spade cards. We shall learn that this almost invariably applies when your four cards include a possible winner and, to the surprise of many, very often when they do not!

It will usually be safe to discard cards in excess of four, but we shall again learn that even here, there can be exceptions. We shall see that your discarding can be a mine of information to declarer and a top-class player will tap it to the full. What is not so well known is that discards by declarer (from his own hand and from dummy) can also be a mine of information to the defenders. It is sad to note that, with the considerable volume of bridge literature on the market, little or nothing has been written on the subject of discarding by declarer. I intend to rectify this here in the closing chapter.

The bulk of the book, however, will be devoted to discards by defenders. For many players, this means signalling to partner, typically giving information like:

    a) encouragement or discouragement of a suit,
    b) count, odd or even,
    c) suit preference in various styles like McKenney, odd and even or
       revolving,
    d) other information like solid holdings.

This area – defensive signalling – was discussed in detail in my book *Signal Success in Bridge*. In his excellent, more recent book, *Step by Step Signalling*, Mark Horton added some new ideas. This book will be devoted to situations where you have the opportunity to ruff and where you have to discard under pressure. To many readers, this will suggest a long discussion on squeezes which is beyond them and they can survive at a reasonable standard without worrying about an aspect of the game best left to the experts. For completeness, however, there will be some discussion on squeeze defence and we shall learn that, even if you are genuinely squeezed, you can still make life a nightmare for declarer, but here I am primarily concerned with far more common positions where you have a winning discard available.

In each chapte there will be worked examples and then some exercises will be offered which I should like you to do under 'exam conditions', i.e. imagine you were playing in a serious game. You will be invited not only to choose your discard, but also to justify it, stating how you think the unseen cards are lying and how you expect the remaining play to go.

I hope you will enjoy it.

Chapter 1

To Ruff or Not to Ruff

Nothing seems to be more thrilling for a defender than to make a trick with a lowly little trump at the expense of a much bigger card belonging to the enemy. Unfortunately, the temptation is sometimes too hot to resist and, notably when sitting under the big card, in second or third position, it can be unwise and indeed costly to ruff.

This is a typical example where, as declarer, I was presented with a completely hopeless game:

East/West Vulnerable. Dealer South.

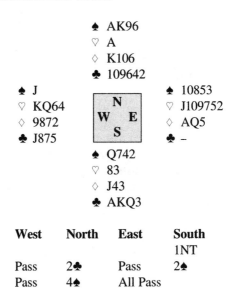

```
              ♠ AK96
              ♡ A
              ◇ K106
              ♣ 109642
  ♠ J          ┌─────────┐      ♠ 10853
  ♡ KQ64       │    N    │      ♡ J109752
  ◇ 9872       │ W     E │      ◇ AQ5
  ♣ J875       │    S    │      ♣ -
               └─────────┘
              ♠ Q742
              ♡ 83
              ◇ J43
              ♣ AKQ3
```

West	North	East	South
			1NT
Pass	2♣	Pass	2♠
Pass	4♠	All Pass	

South's opener showed 12-14 points and a Stayman sequence followed.

West led the ◇9. East won with the ◇Q, cashed the ◇A and played a third round, putting dummy on play. As declarer, I realised that the contract was only in danger if both black suits misbehaved, specifically if West held all the outstanding clubs offside. So I played a club from dummy immediately, tempting East with the poisoned bait. East ruffed in and that was the end; I was able to take the rest.

East had committed a number of cardinal sins, which can be summed up in the following tip:

Guiding Principle

Be reluctant to ruff in second or third position in front of high cards. Very often that will amount to:

a) ruffing partner's trick, which is effectively
b) winning the same trick twice over
c) weakening the defenders' trump holding for no material gain.

It is usually right to ruff *after* the high card has been played.

In the above example, East was particularly ill-advised to ruff in because, in the knowledge that his partner had a singleton trump, he should have realised that, if it were an honour, the partnership was now worth a natural trump trick. In that case, there was no need to ruff. Even if there were no natural trump trick, declarer would have to draw four rounds to clear the trumps, which might prove expensive. Usually, at worst, the defenders will break even by refusing to ruff. They will seldom lose. Here East had quite a strong trump holding, but we shall learn later that even very poor holdings may be worth keeping for other reasons. One of those is to avoid revealing the trump position. In this next hand, East demonstrated an alarming lack of awareness of what was going on:

North/South Game. Dealer West.

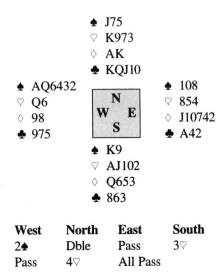

♠ J75			
♡ K973			
◇ AK			
♣ KQJ10			

West	North	East	South
West	**North**	**East**	**South**
2♠	Dble	Pass	3♡
Pass	4♡	All Pass	

After West's weak two opening (about 5-9 points with six spades) and North's take-out double, North/South were employing a variant of the Lebensohl convention whereby the reply of 3♡ showed some values. Had South wanted to bid hearts on a very weak hand, he would have bid a forcing 2NT and, after the requested 3♣ response from North, he would then have bid 3♡, indicating a weak hand – say seven or fewer points.

Playing a middle-up-down or 'MUD' lead style, West started with the ♣7, won by East's ♣A. The ♠10 was returned, won by West's ♠Q and he then cashed the ♠A before exiting in diamonds. Dummy won perforce and now declarer called for the now established ♣J. With obviously 'hopeless' trumps, East ruffed. South overruffed and now, confident that East had nothing to hide, played West for the ♡Q, making the contract in comfort.

Certainly there are cases where one should ruff in this kind of situation, but surely only if declarer is threatening to discard a loser. Here, with dummy's minor-suit holdings rock solid, there are surely no losers to discard and all declarer was trying to do was to get free trump information; East duly obliged. If East refuses to ruff, declarer, knowing that spades are 6-2, is far more likely to play East for the ♡Q – one off.

There are two tips stemming from this hand:

Guiding Principle

When offered a ruff in this kind of situation, be sure you understand what declarer is trying to achieve before accepting or declining.

Guiding Principle

When looking at a poor trump holding, consider the trump strength of the defensive partnership as a whole rather than your own hand alone.

We shall learn later, when we discuss parity, that this does not only apply to trumps. Selfishness of this kind has no place at the bridge table.

Having tried to put you off ruffing for good, I must now rectify matters by showing you situations where you must ruff even if it is obvious that you are going to be overruffed. Here is a hand where nobody less than a grand master went wrong:

East/West Game. Dealer South.

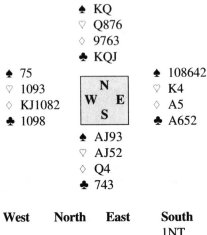

♠	KQ
♡	Q876
♢	9763
♣	KQJ

♠ 75		♠ 108642
♡ 1093		♡ K4
♢ KJ1082		♢ A5
♣ 1098		♣ A652

♠	AJ93
♡	AJ52
♢	Q4
♣	743

West	North	East	South
			1NT
Pass	2♣	Pass	2♡
Pass	4♡	All Pass	

A Stayman sequence followed a 12-14 point opening.

As West, I led the ♣10, won by East. On the ♢A, I encouraged with the ♢J and East continued with a second round which I won with the ♢K. I now returned the ♢2, forcing partner to ruff. He did – with the ♡4!! – contract made. East clearly did not ask himself what was going on. What was I trying to achieve? He knew that I had three trumps in my hand and in no circumstances could it cost to ruff high. Nothing now could prevent my ♡10 from scoring the setting trick. This idea of a defender with shortage in trumps ruffing as high as possible to force declarer to use higher trumps, thus promoting tricks for his partner, is called an 'uppercut' and occurs more often than many players realise.

The converse of this is that defenders can also promote their trumps by refusing to overruff. This is a common situation:

Game All. Dealer East.

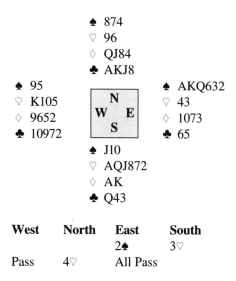

	♠ 874		
	♡ 96		
	◊ QJ84		
	♣ AKJ8		

♠ 95   ♠ AKQ632
♡ K105   ♡ 43
◊ 9652   ◊ 1073
♣ 10972   ♣ 65

♠ J10
♡ AQJ872
◊ AK
♣ Q43

West	North	East	South
		2♠	3♡
Pass	4♡	All Pass	

East bid a weak two, about 5-9 points and a six-card suit.

West led his partner's suit and East cashed two top winners. On the third round South ruffed with the ♡J and West overruffed with the ♡K. That was three tricks, but the defenders could take no more. Now observe the effect of West's discarding a minor-suit card at trick three. All of a sudden:

♡ K105

♡ AQJ872

where it appears the defender can expect one trick only, has become:

♡ K105

♡ AQ872

after which nothing can prevent West from taking two tricks.

So we have seen a number of examples, in some of which it is right to ruff while, in others, it is very costly. To decide which is right, the defender has to consider what his side and the enemy are trying to achieve. That is the decision you will have to take in each of the following ten examples. Once your moment comes, you must decide whether to ruff high, low or not at all and, far more important, why! Take no credit for good guesswork.

Quiz on when to ruff

Problem 1.1
Game All. Dealer East.

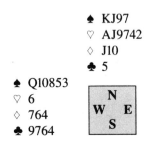

♠ KJ97
♡ AJ9742
◊ J10
♣ 5

♠ Q10853
♡ 6
◊ 764
♣ 9764

West	North	East	South
		1◊	1NT
Pass	2♣	Dble	2♠
Pass	4♠	All Pass	

You lead the ◊6 and partner cashes the ◊K and ◊A while South follows with the ◊3 and ◊5 and you play the ◊7(MUD style) to show a third card. Partner switches to the ♣Q, won by South with the ♣A. He cashes the ♠A, on which partner discards the ♣2. A second round of trumps is won by dummy's ♠9, partner discarding a diamond. All follow to the ♡K, partner playing the ♡5, and now South plays the ♡8. How do you defend?

Problem 1.2
Game All. Dealer South.

♠ KJ1073
♡ 872
◊ K43
♣ QJ

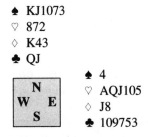

♠ 4
♡ AQJ105
◊ J8
♣ 109753

West	North	East	South
			2NT
Pass	3♡	Dble	4♠
Pass	5♣	Pass	6♠
All Pass			

North transferred to spades, enabling East to double for the lead. The disadvantage of this was that South was now able to upgrade his ♡K and he decided to break the transfer.

Partner leads the ♡9 to the ♡2, ♡A and ♡3. You return the ♡Q, South winning with the ♡K as West follows with the ♡6. South cashes the ◊A and ◊Q, partner following with the ◊6 and ◊2, and crosses to dummy with the ♣Q, all following, and now plays the ◊K. How do you defend?

Problem 1.3
North/South Game. Dealer South.

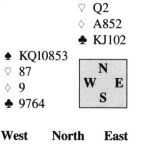

♠	762
♡	Q2
◊	A852
♣	KJ102

| ♠ KQ10853 |
| ♡ 87 |
| ◊ 9 |
| ♣ 9764 |

West	North	East	South
			1♡
2♠	Dble	3♠	4♡
All Pass			

You lead your singleton diamond to the ◊2, ◊3 and ◊K. A trump goes to dummy's ♡Q and partner's ♡A. He continues with the ◊Q, South following with the ◊4. How do you defend?

Problem 1.4
North/South Game. Dealer West.

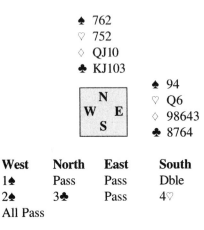

| ♠ 762 |
| ♡ 752 |
| ◇ QJ10 |
| ♣ KJ103 |

West	North	East	South
1♠	Pass	Pass	Dble
2♠	3♣	Pass	4♡
All Pass			

Partner leads out the ♠A and ♠K; you peter, while South follows with the ♠10 and ♠J. Partner now cashes the ◇A, all following low, and then plays the ♠3 to dummy's ♠7. Have you any comment on the play so far and how do you defend?

Problem 1.5
Game All. Dealer South.

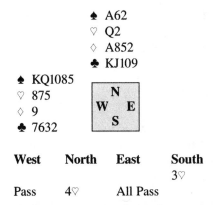

West	North	East	South
			3♡
Pass	4♡	All Pass	

You lead your ◇9 to the ◇2, ◇3 and ◇K. South continues with the ♣Q and you give count with the ♣6. Dummy overtakes and partner wins with the

♣A. He returns the ◇10 and South plays the ◇6. How do you defend?

Problem 1.6
North/South Game. Dealer West.

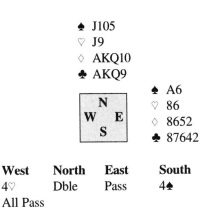

　　　　　　　　♠ J105
　　　　　　　　♡ J9
　　　　　　　　◇ AKQ10
　　　　　　　　♣ AKQ9
　　　　　　　　　　　　　♠ A6
　　　　　　　　　　　　　♡ 86
　　　　　　　　　　　　　◇ 8652
　　　　　　　　　　　　　♣ 87642

West	**North**	**East**	**South**
4♡	Dble	Pass	4♠
All Pass			

North's double shows a generally good hand, rather than being specifically for penalties or take-out. Most partnerships nowadays agree that a double of 4♡ shows a willingness to play in 4♠.

West leads the ♡A and ♡K, all following as you peter. Now follows the ♡5 and dummy's ♠J is played. How do you defend?

Problem 1.7
Love All. Dealer North.

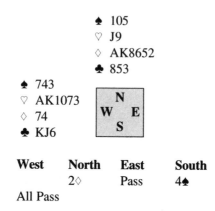

	♠ 105
	♡ J9
	◊ AK8652
	♣ 853

♠ 743
♡ AK1073
◊ 74
♣ KJ6

West	North	East	South
	2◊	Pass	4♠
All Pass			

North/South were playing weak twos in all non-club suits.

You lead the two top hearts, partner following with ♡6 and ♡8, while declarer contributes the ♡4 and ♡Q. The heart position is curious. Since the ♡5 and ♡2 are missing, it looks as if partner *began* to peter in hearts, but is now trying to show you that his only useful values are in diamonds rather than clubs. It may well be that you need to attack the diamond position to cut declarer's communications before trumps are drawn. You therefore judge well to switch to a diamond and declarer cashes the ◊A and ◊K before playing a third round. Partner follows with the ◊9, ◊Q, ◊J while South plays the ◊3 and ◊10 and then ruffs with the ♠2. How do you defend?

Problem 1.8
East/West Game. Dealer South.

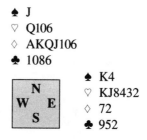

♠ J
♡ Q106
◊ AKQJ106
♣ 1086

♠ K4
♡ KJ8432
◊ 72
♣ 952

West	North	East	South
			1♠
Pass	2◇	Pass	4♠
Pass	4NT	Pass	5♠
Pass	6♠	All Pass	

This was a typical agricultural auction you get at club duplicates and tournaments. Lacking second-round control in two suits, North's hand is grossly unsuitable for Blackwood, but, once he found his partner with three aces and presumably very strong spades, the slam is certainly not unreasonable.

Partner leads the ♣K, won by the ♣A in the South hand. The ◇8 is covered by partner's ◇9 and won by the ◇A in dummy. On the second high diamond, South discards the ♣3. Now the ◇Q is played. How do you defend?

Problem 1.9
Game All. Dealer East.

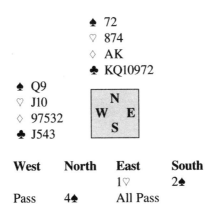

```
              ♠ 72
              ♡ 874
              ◇ AK
              ♣ KQ10972
  ♠ Q9
  ♡ J10          N
  ◇ 97532    W       E
  ♣ J543         S
```

West	North	East	South
		1♡	2♠
Pass	4♠	All Pass	

South's jump overcall was of intermediate strength.

You lead the ♡J and partner cashes the ♡K and ♡A as South follows with the ♡5 and ♡Q. On the ♡9, South ruffs with the ♠J. How do you defend?

Problem 1.10
Game All. Dealer East.

           ♠ K10986
           ♡ AJ
           ◇ AJ
           ♣ AK109

♠ AQ
♡ KQ10864
◇ 74
♣ 742

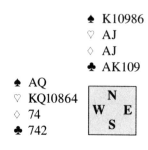

West	North	East	South
		Pass	Pass
1♡	Dble	Pass	2♠
Pass	6♠	All Pass	

As you see, North is not one for scientific bidding, but he has realised that cards are likely to be well placed for him.

You lead the ♡K, won in dummy as East plays the ♡2 and South the ♡3. Dummy's ◇A is cashed and another diamond is won by South's ◇K, partner following with the ◇5 and ◇2. Now he plays the ◇Q. How do you defend?

Solutions

Problem 1.1

As you have longer trumps than either North or South, you are bound to make at least one trump trick and there is no hurry to take it. If you ruff now, not only are you prematurely and unnecessarily weakening your trump holding, but it is likely that you are ruffing partner's heart trick, effectively winning the same trick twice over. The deal:

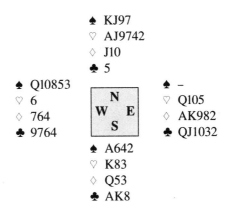

```
                    ♠ KJ97
                    ♡ AJ9742
                    ◇ J10
                    ♣ 5
    ♠ Q10853      ┌─────────┐      ♠ –
    ♡ 6           │   N     │      ♡ Q105
    ◇ 764         │ W     E │      ◇ AK982
    ♣ 9764        │   S     │      ♣ QJ1032
                  └─────────┘
                    ♠ A642
                    ♡ K83
                    ◇ Q53
                    ♣ AK8
```

Just discard a minor-suit card patiently and you will allow partner to make his ♡Q in the fullness of time and note that, even if declarer's hearts are solid, you achieve nothing by ruffing. If you ruff, you will have to play a minor-suit card afterwards (or a trump, doing declarer's work for him) after which your remaining trumps can be picked up with a finesse. Yet the number of people who would ruff in this situation is alarming.

Problem 1.2

Obviously declarer is trying to discard his heart loser so it looks as though you must ruff with your 'useless' trump to prevent this. Is that right? Nonsense! What was the big rush? Why did he not draw trumps first? A roll-call on points will keep you on the right track here. There are ten in dummy and eight in your hand. That means, even restricting South to a minimum twenty, partner can have no more than a queen. Thus, known to have both top club honours, declarer could easily discard dummy's losing heart on the clubs after drawing trumps. No, declarer is trying to con you into helping him solve another problem:

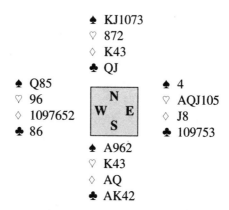

```
              ♠ KJ1073
              ♡ 872
              ◇ K43
              ♣ QJ
  ♠ Q85                      ♠ 4
  ♡ 96         ┌────────┐    ♡ AQJ105
  ◇ 1097652    │   N    │    ◇ J8
  ♣ 86         │ W    E │    ♣ 109753
               │   S    │
               └────────┘
              ♠ A962
              ♡ K43
              ◇ AQ
              ♣ AK42
```

Where is the ♠Q? If you ruff, you give the show away. If you do not, declarer knows that you have five hearts and two diamonds against partner's two hearts and six diamonds. Thus, if anything, the trump queen is more likely to be with East. He can still play for the drop, but if you discard a club or a heart on this trick, the chances are that he will go down. Admittedly, declarer took a slight risk with this line of play: there may have been a 7-1 diamond split or West may have a doubleton. But in the light of the bidding, these are unlikely and it was surely, percentage-wise, worthwhile to make every effort to get you to help him solve the crucial problem of the hand.

Problem 1.3

This is another situation where fools rush in. It is obvious from the early play that partner's diamonds are solid from queen down and by ruffing, you are merely ruffing his trick. However, if you discard and allow dummy's ◇A to win, not only do you set up winners in the suit for partner as here:

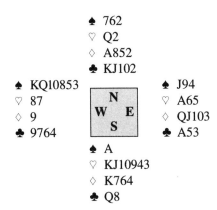

♠ 762
♥ Q2
♦ A852
♣ KJ102

♠ KQ10853
♥ 87
♦ 9
♣ 9764

♠ J94
♥ A65
♦ QJ103
♣ A53

♠ A
♥ KJ10943
♦ K764
♣ Q8

but you also insist that the ♦A is removed from the scene early. If you ruff and allow it to stay in dummy, it will serve as an entry to the clubs and declarer will be able to discard his diamond loser on that suit, making the contract with five hearts, one spade, two diamonds and two clubs. On my recommended defence, you will follow up by giving partner a count in clubs and now declarer is restricted to five hearts, a spade, one club and two diamonds – only nine tricks.

Problem 1.4

Partner is clearly trying to arrange a trump promotion and you should cooperate by ruffing as high as you can, here with the ♥Q. This promotes partner's ♥J in this layout:

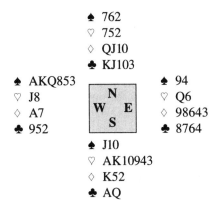

♠ 762
♥ 752
♦ QJ10
♣ KJ103

♠ AKQ853
♥ J8
♦ A7
♣ 952

♠ 94
♥ Q6
♦ 98643
♣ 8764

♠ J10
♥ AK10943
♦ K52
♣ AQ

You should have commented on the early cashing of the ♦A. This never costs and is necessary if South proves to be 2614. Now he can counter your plans by discarding his losing diamond on your ♡Q, effectively a loser-on-loser play. Once partner cashes his ◊A, South has no loser to discard and must go down.

Problem 1.5

This looks similar to Problem 1.3, but there are differences. Here there is no time to stand on ceremony. South is trying to discard potential diamond losers on those clubs and there is no time to lose. You must ruff and get partner in quickly. There is no hope in spades with the ♠A on view and it has to be trumps. Declarer has already shown the ◊K and ♣Q and did not draw trumps immediately which all strongly suggests that partner is likely to hold the ♡A. You should have ruffed with a high trump and then returned a lower one, confirming that you have a third available for another ruff. The deal:

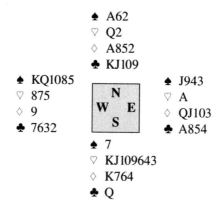

```
              ♠ A62
              ♡ Q2
              ◊ A852
              ♣ KJ109
♠ KQ1085                      ♠ J943
♡ 875           N             ♡ A
◊ 9         W       E         ◊ QJ103
♣ 7632          S             ♣ A854
              ♠ 7
              ♡ KJ109643
              ◊ K764
              ♣ Q
```

Note partner's excellent carding in diamonds: 10 from QJ10 trying to get you to do the right thing. Had he played the queen, it still would have been right for you to ruff. It cannot cost to do so with the ♠A being an obvious entry to dummy and the clubs threatening.

From this problem and Problem 1.3, we can lay down a tip:

Guiding Principle
While it is usually wrong to ruff in front of winners, it is likely to be right if you can arrange to do so twice. Also consider the likelihood of declarer's losers being discarded early as in 1.5.

Problem 1.6

Partner's deliberately low heart is a clear indication that he wants you to ruff and you should hit it as hard as you can. You should overruff with the ♠A, promoting partner's ♠Q in this lay-out:

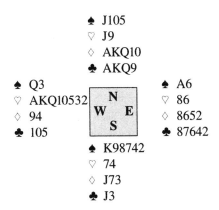

```
                    ♠ J105
                    ♡ J9
                    ◊ AKQ10
                    ♣ AKQ9
        ♠ Q3                        ♠ A6
        ♡ AKQ10532    N             ♡ 86
        ◊ 94        W   E           ◊ 8652
        ♣ 105          S            ♣ 87642
                    ♠ K98742
                    ♡ 74
                    ◊ J73
                    ♣ J3
```

If you fail to do so, declarer will be able to lead a low trump from dummy towards his ♠K, picking up the trumps for the loss of only one trick. Note that partner offered declarer a ruff and discard here, but that was very much in order when two conditions are satisfied. These can be summed up in the following tip:

Guiding Principle

While giving away a ruff and discard is regarded by many as one of the worst offences that a defender can commit, it is almost invariably the right defence if the following two conditions apply:

a) Declarer has no losers to discard, i.e. he cannot materially benefit from the 'extra' trick, and

b) his prime weakness is his trump holding which needs to be attacked at all costs.

Problem 1.7

This seems to be a little bit strange. Having bid 4♠ on his own, with no guarantee of support from his partner, South surely has tremendous trumps and yet all he could manage was the ♠2! Clearly you have little hope of making any of your trumps so it seems obvious to overruff gratefully and exit with a trump, carefully avoiding opening up the clubs or giving a ruff and discard with a heart continuation.

However, before falling headlong into the trap, it might pay to consider what is going to happen then. A roll-call on the trump suit will keep your head above water. Declarer surely has at least six and his early play clearly indicates that he is trying to set up the diamond suit. If you overruff on this trick, you bring your trump length down to North's and now South will be able to draw trumps ending in dummy (the crucial point), after which he will be able to cash the long diamonds, discarding his club losers. Did you notice how partner followed to those diamonds? The ◊Q followed by the ◊J, the unusual order, carried a message that he was unable to help you in clubs. Look out for these no-cost signals.

If you hold on to your three trumps, dummy's diamonds cannot be used. You will forego the trump trick offered, but get two club tricks in return. The correct defence is to discard a heart:

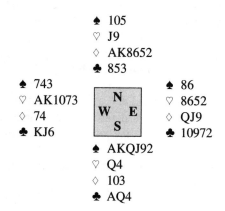

```
                    ♠ 105
                    ♡ J9
                    ◊ AK8652
                    ♣ 853
    ♠ 743                         ♠ 86
    ♡ AK1073      N               ♡ 8652
    ◊ 74        W   E             ◊ QJ9
    ♣ KJ6         S               ♣ 10972
                    ♠ AKQJ92
                    ♡ Q4
                    ◊ 103
                    ♣ AQ4
```

Problem 1.8

Clearly, if you ruff, you will be giving up all hope of a trump trick, while if you refuse to ruff, declarer will continue to discard losers in clubs and/or hearts and now you may (or may not) get a trump trick, but no more. Thus you must hope that partner has enough to beat this contract in clubs and/or hearts and prevent any further discards by ruffing in now. Is there any point in ruffing high? This might promote a trump trick for partner is he has, say, ♠10xx. No – the cost is too great. South will overruff and now be able to cross back to dummy with the ♠J, play yet another high diamond, (remember partner is still following) and throw another loser, which will probably be critical, as here:

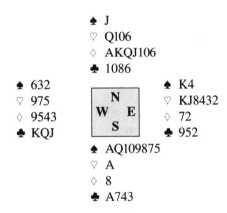

```
                      ♠ J
                      ♡ Q106
                      ◇ AKQJ106
                      ♣ 1086
     ♠ 632                              ♠ K4
     ♡ 975            ┌─────────┐       ♡ KJ8432
     ◇ 9543           │    N    │       ◇ 72
     ♣ KQJ            │  W   E  │       ♣ 952
                      │    S    │
                      └─────────┘
                      ♠ AQ109875
                      ♡ A
                      ◇ 8
                      ♣ A743
```

The only effective defence is to ruff with the ♠4. Dummy is now cut off permanently and West will wait for his two club tricks.

Problem 1.9

It seems obvious to overruff with the ♠Q, which may be a loser otherwise, but it is wrong for two reasons. Did you ask yourself what the trump situation was? Even if declarer has all the big trumps apart from the queen, declining to overruff is unlikely to cost. Declarer will note that you were 'unable' to do so and play your partner for it anyway, losing the finesse. Overruffing definitely costs if South's trumps are weaker, as here:

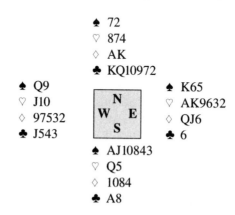

Now declarer can cross to dummy twice in diamonds to take finesses against partner's ♠K and will lose no further tricks. But if you just discard a minor-suit card now, nothing can prevent your gaining two trump tricks. Effectively you have promoted that ♠9 by refusing to overruff.

Problem 1.10

This seems terrible as declarer is threatening to discard dummy's ♡J, his only non-trump loser. To refuse to ruff amounts to throwing in the towel immediately. South will play a trump and cannot go wrong. To ruff with the ♠A is no better, the discard can still be made. The only defence is to accept that your ♠Q never had a chance anyway and treat it as a loser. Ruff with the ♠Q and North has to overruff after which you can quietly wait for one trick in each major:

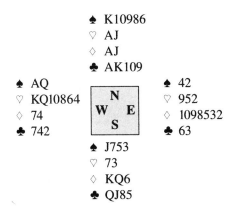

```
                    ♠ K10986
                    ♡ AJ
                    ◇ AJ
                    ♣ AK109
    ♠ AQ          ┌─────────┐      ♠ 42
    ♡ KQ10864     │    N    │      ♡ 952
    ◇ 74          │  W   E  │      ◇ 1098532
    ♣ 742         │    S    │      ♣ 63
                  └─────────┘
                    ♠ J753
                    ♡ 73
                    ◇ KQ6
                    ♣ QJ85
```

If you got that right, you can than sit back and listen to the opponents' post-mortem in which they will try to establish why they were not playing in an impregnable 6♣!

We are now going to turn to situations where you have to discard under pressure and lay down guidelines for minimising the damage.

Chapter 2

Maintaining Parity

It will be appropriate to start this section with a basic tip mentioned earlier:

Guiding Principle

If it is clear that a specific number of rounds of a suit will be played, keep that number of cards: definitely if they include a potential winner, probably if they do not. It will usually be safe to discard any extras, but even then be careful.

So firstly, we have to decide how many rounds of each suit will be played. As already indicated, opponents' bidding and declarer's early play will often be a useful guide. This hand came up recently:

East/West Game. Dealer East.

```
                    ♠ 86
                    ♡ 9743
                    ◇ KQ3
                    ♣ AQ108
        ♠ K103          N           ♠ Q752
        ♡ K106      W       E       ♡ Q852
        ◇ J10987        S           ◇ 4
        ♣ KJ                        ♣ 9743
                    ♠ AJ94
                    ♡ AJ
                    ◇ A652
                    ♣ 652
```

West	North	East	South
		Pass	1NT
Pass	2♣	Pass	2♠
Pass	2NT	Pass	3NT
All Pass			

West led the ◊J, won in dummy. Declarer ran the ♠8 round to West's ♠10 and West persisted with the ◊10. Dummy won again and East had to discard. He chose a 'useless' club, presenting declarer with an extra trick in that suit and the contract. Should he have known better? Clearly, as declarer attacked spades with a minority and lost to the ♠10, he will probably be fairly strong in the suit and it would be folly to discard from it. But what is the club position? If declarer has both ♣K and ♣J, four tricks would be available and there will be no harm in East's keeping his holding. The critical case arises when West has one or both club honours, in which case East's ♣9 will be promotable. A better discard is a heart. As we shall see later, declarer is not down yet, but a club discard gives him an easy nine tricks.

A similar principle applied in the following hand where a defender refused to discard from Qxx. He could see the king and jack, but failed to ask himself about the rest of the hand.

Love All. Dealer East.

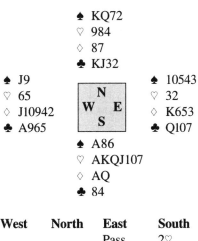

```
              ♠ KQ72
              ♡ 984
              ◊ 87
              ♣ KJ32
♠ J9                        ♠ 10543
♡ 65          N             ♡ 32
◊ J10942    W   E           ◊ K653
♣ A965        S             ♣ Q107
              ♠ A86
              ♡ AKQJ107
              ◊ AQ
              ♣ 84
```

West	North	East	South
		Pass	2♡
Pass	4♡	Pass	4♠
Pass	5♣	Pass	6♡
All Pass			

South felt he had a little extra on top of his announced eight playing tricks. North's 4♡ showed a positive response, but no ace so that his cue-bid of 5♣ showed second-round control.

Against this rather optimistic contract, West led the ◊J to the ◊7, ◊6 and

◊Q and now five rounds of trumps followed, West following twice and then discarding three diamonds. Two clubs were discarded from dummy. East too let go of three diamonds, but then, on the ◊A, still to play to this trick, he could see:

♠ KQ72
♡ –
◊ –
♣ KJ

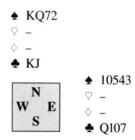

♠ 10543
♡ –
◊ –
♣ Q107

A black card had to go. East discarded a spade and declarer had no further problem.

When declarer played out trumps, it was clear that he started with two diamonds only. With more, he could easily have arranged for a ruff in dummy. Thus it was clear that only two rounds of diamonds were going to be played and both defenders were correct in discarding, having no hope of a trick in that suit. South's bidding clarified that he had the ♠A and thus was in a position to play four rounds of the suit. In that case, a spade discard from East would allow South four tricks to go with six hearts and two diamonds for the contract without touching clubs.

Clearly, therefore, partner had to be credited with the ♣A for there to be any hope at all, so the 'rule' of not discarding from Qxx does not apply; East can safely come down to Qx, leaving South to guess. As it was, South claimed without sweat. It is worth emphasising the importance of roll-calling in this hand. I could have made the problem harder by allowing South to shut his eyes and 'bash' 6♡ without informative cue-bidding. Now, as far as East is concerned, it is not clear what the black-suit position is.

Suppose he tries to work it out on the evidence. He knows about six solid hearts, ten points and the ◊AQ, another six to total sixteen so far. If South had both black aces, that would imply twenty-four and a 2♣ opener so that is ruled out. If he has the ♣A, but not the ♠A, declarer can easily make his contract, irrespective of his black-suit length and it will be instructive to prove this. With a doubleton or more, he simply leads twice towards dummy and ensures two spade tricks to go with six hearts, two diamonds and two top clubs. With a singleton in a 1633 distribution, he simply leads towards dummy once and West can choose his poison. If he ducks, South plays on clubs, losing to East's queen, but making the contract when the suit breaks

3-3. If he wins, South does have two spade tricks after all.

For that reason, East must judge that West needs the ♣A for the defenders to have any significant chance and must discard a low club as indicated above.

I have gone into great detail with this hand because it illustrates a very common situation in which players, even up to good county standard, continually go wrong.

In this next example, the number of rounds of a suit expected is crucial again even though the defender knows that his 'winner' is going to be ruffed:

Love All. Dealer West.

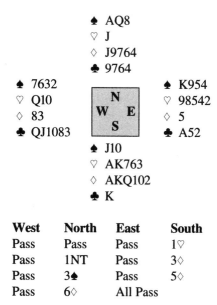

```
                    ♠ AQ8
                    ♡ J
                    ◇ J9764
                    ♣ 9764
   ♠ 7632                          ♠ K954
   ♡ Q10          N                ♡ 98542
   ◇ 83       W       E            ◇ 5
   ♣ QJ1083         S              ♣ A52
                    ♠ J10
                    ♡ AK763
                    ◇ AKQ102
                    ♣ K
```

West	North	East	South
Pass	Pass	Pass	1♡
Pass	1NT	Pass	3◇
Pass	3♠	Pass	5◇
Pass	6◇	All Pass	

North has done well to keep options open with 3♠, but, once his partner signed off in 5◇, he should have accepted the decision.

West led the ♣Q, East winning. It was apparent to East that a big crossruff was threatened so he switched to his trump, won by South. The ♡A and a low heart followed, West dropping the ♡10 and ♡Q as dummy ruffed. Now came a second trump and East had to discard. The low hearts seemed worthless so he threw one, presenting South with an unmakeable contract. The ♡K and the established fifth heart accounted for dummy's two losing spades. East should have realised that his black-suit holdings were of no use and thrown one of those instead. The hearts, with South known to have five, were gold-dust and, had he kept control of the fifth round, South would have been at the mercy of the spade position, failing on the lie of the cards. It was argued afterwards that East could have saved embarrassment by doubling 3♠ for a lead. However, warned of trouble ahead, it is likely that South would now have stopped in a cold 5◇. In my experience, it usually pays to keep quiet in these situations, but you have to defend correctly.

We have, so far, looked at positions where the roll-call is fairly clear. On many occasions, it is more obscure and now the seven roll-calls have to be used in unison to find the lay-out which will give the defenders a chance. On the following deal, a grand master went astray because he failed to place the unseen cards accurately:

East/West Game. Dealer East.

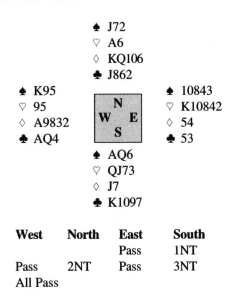

```
                    ♠ J72
                    ♡ A6
                    ◇ KQ106
                    ♣ J862
      ♠ K95                        ♠ 10843
      ♡ 95          N              ♡ K10842
      ◇ A9832    W     E           ◇ 54
      ♣ AQ4         S              ♣ 53
                    ♠ AQ6
                    ♡ QJ73
                    ◇ J7
                    ♣ K1097
```

West	North	East	South
		Pass	1NT
Pass	2NT	Pass	3NT
All Pass			

West lead the ◇3, won in dummy. The ♣8 was run to West's ♣Q and a second diamond, the deuce, was won in hand. The ♣K was won by West's ♣A and he cashed the ◇A and played the ◇9, won in dummy. East could easily discard a heart on the third round of diamonds, but on the fourth another major-suit card had to go. He chose another heart, allowing South three heart tricks and the contract.

We shall do the seven roll-calls and see what we can find out. We know that South started with a good 13-14 points, a doubleton ◇J and the ♣K, four points so far. He will clearly make two club tricks and three diamonds, five to date.

Partner obviously started with ◊A9832 and East should have noted that his fourth round was the ◊9 rather than the ◊8, suggesting interest in the higher-ranking major, spades. It was thus more important for West to guard hearts and his second discard should have been in spades. That would allow declarer two tricks in hearts and one in spades, but hopefully no more. If he allowed West in, with a view to making a second spade trick, partner could cash a long diamond to defeat the contract.

This hand is not easy, but it shows what type of thinking is required. So far, we have seen that the defender must keep winners or potential winners rather than losers. Sometimes, almost incredibly, the loser must be allowed priority. In this next hand, defenders almost invariably bow to declarer's wishes simply because they forget they have a partner:

Game All. Dealer North.

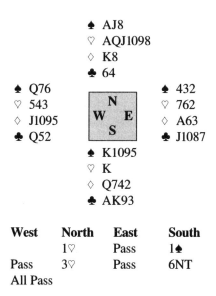

	♠ AJ8	
	♡ AQJ1098	
	◊ K8	
	♣ 64	
♠ Q76		♠ 432
♡ 543		♡ 762
◊ J1095		◊ A63
♣ Q52		♣ J1087
	♠ K1095	
	♡ K	
	◊ Q742	
	♣ AK93	

West	North	East	South
	1♡	Pass	1♠
Pass	3♡	Pass	6NT
All Pass			

Following this stunning display of agricultural bidding, West led the ◊J, covered in dummy and won by East. The suit was continued, South winning. Now followed six rounds of hearts. South discarded two diamonds, a spade and a club on the second to fifth rounds. East could easily follow three times and discard his last diamond on the fourth round, but after that two more rejects were needed. Looking at that devastating spade holding, a second thought was hardly needed. When he discarded two spades, South gratefully placed the ♠Q with West and finessed accordingly to make the contract.

Again, the seven roll-calls would have saved East an embarrassing post-mortem. South was clearly good for six hearts tricks and one diamond, seven so far. Obviously he needs the ♣A to have any chance at all to total eight. This meant that he either had to bring in the spades for four tricks or he needed more top clubs. He had already thrown one club; thus, if his remaining clubs were ♣AKQ, East's holding was irrelevant. If they were AKx, West still had control of the suit. The critical suit was spades. South had bid them and thrown one so he still had another three at least. He would need the king or queen to have any chance and, if he had both, the contract was cold. The critical position arose when he had the king but not the queen. Now, if he did not hold the ten, he would have only one way to finesse, the right way, and the contract was unbeatable. The crucial position arose when he did have the ten; now a two-way guess would be available. It was up to East to hold his spades to give maximum encouragement for declarer to go wrong. The correct discards were clubs. Now West keeps parity with declarer according to South's discards, leaving South to guess. If South discards two spades, he effectively commits himself to finessing against East.

In practice, what East did was to discard from a critical holding of the *partnership*. So we can now table our second guiding principle which will hopefully cure defenders from their phobia of discarding from Kx, Qxx, Jxxx etc.

Guiding Principle

When considering discarding from potentially embarrassing holdings, consider that of the partnership as a whole.

Thus, while discarding from Kx may cost if partner has nothing, it is safe if partner has the queen, (unless of course, she too is alone). Similarly, you can throw from Qxx if partner is as good as Jxx or from Jxxx if partner has the queen or better.

This principle is crucial to all problems in discarding.

I should like you now to do some examples in match conditions.

Quiz on parity

Problem 2.1
Game All. Dealer South.

♠ 1086
♡ AQ75
◇ 32
♣ A764

♠ Q743
♡ 8432
◇ 76
♣ K108

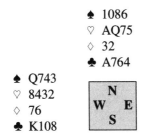

West	North	East	South
			2◇
Pass	2NT	Pass	4◇
Pass	4♡	Pass	4♠
Pass	5♣	Pass	6◇
All Pass			

After a strong Acol two by South, 2♡ would have been a Herbert negative so 2NT was positive and balanced. The 4◇ bid showed a solid suit and demanded cue-bidding.

You decide to lead a safe-looking trump and declarer draws three rounds, partner following with the ◇4, ◇5, ◇9, while you discard the ♠7. Declarer now plays a fourth round of diamonds. What do you discard? (Note that declarer still has two more diamonds)

Problem 2.2
Love All. Dealer East.

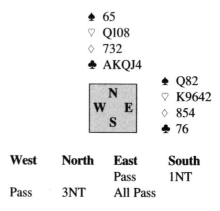

```
            ♠ 65
            ♡ Q108
            ◇ 732
            ♣ AKQJ4
                          ♠ Q82
              N           ♡ K9642
           W     E        ◇ 854
              S           ♣ 76
```

West	North	East	South
		Pass	1NT
Pass	3NT	All Pass	

South's opener showed 12-14 points.

West leads the ♠10 to the ♠5, ♠Q and ♠K. On the first round of clubs, West, with count clearly irrelevant, plays the ♣10, emphasising spades and, on the second round, the ♣9. More clubs are coming; how do you plan your discards?

Problem 2.3
Game All. Dealer South.

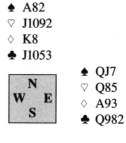

```
            ♠ A82
            ♡ J1092
            ◇ K8
            ♣ J1053
                          ♠ QJ7
              N           ♡ Q85
           W     E        ◇ A93
              S           ♣ Q982
```

West	North	East	South
			1NT
Pass	2♣	Pass	2◇
Pass	2NT	Pass	3NT
All Pass			

South's opener showed 15-17 points and a Stayman sequence followed.

The defenders get off to a flying start when West leads the ◊Q and they take the first four tricks, South having started with ♡7652. Dummy discards two spades. On the fourth round, what should East discard?

Problem 2.4
Game All. Dealer East.

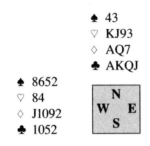

♠ 43
♡ KJ93
◊ AQ7
♣ AKQJ

♠ 8652
♡ 84
◊ J1092
♣ 1052

West	North	East	South
		Pass	1♠
Pass	2♣	Pass	3NT
Pass	7NT	All Pass	

South showed a minimum of 16 points.

You lead the ◊J, won in dummy with the ◊A, East playing the ◊4 and South the ◊8. A low heart goes to partner's ♡10 and South's ♡A and now four rounds of clubs follow. All follow three times; then, on the last round, East discards the ◊5 declarer the ♡2 and, still to play, you can now see:

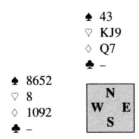

♠ 43
♡ KJ9
◊ Q7
♣ –

♠ 8652
♡ 8
◊ 1092
♣ –

What do you discard?

Problem 2.5
Love All. Dealer East.

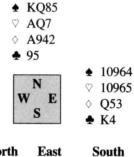

♠ KQ85
♡ AQ7
◊ A942
♣ 95

♠ 10964
♡ 10965
◊ Q53
♣ K4

West	North	East	South
		Pass	1NT
Pass	2♣	Pass	2♡
Pass	3NT	All Pass	

South's opener showed 12-14 points and he was expected to correct 3NT to 4♠ if he had four cards in both majors.

West leads the ♣Q and you overtake, holding the trick. The second round is won by West's ♣10 and he continues with the ♣8. What do you discard?

Problem 2.6
Love All. Dealer East.

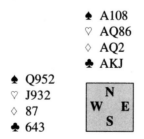

♠ A108
♡ AQ86
◊ AQ2
♣ AKJ

♠ Q952
♡ J932
◊ 87
♣ 643

West	North	East	South
		Pass	1NT
Pass	7NT	All Pass	

South's opener showed 12-14 points.

You lead the ◊8 and South wins with the ◊J in hand, dummy playing the ◊2 and partner the ◊3. Having started with ♣Q1092, declarer now cashes four rounds of clubs. You discard a diamond, dummy discards the ◊A and partner the ◊6. Now follows the ◊K, crashing dummy's ◊Q and you must be prepared for a further round of the suit. What will be your two discards?

Problem 2.7
Game All. Dealer South.

```
          ♠ A1095
          ♡ A
          ◊ AKJ1032
          ♣ J3
♠ K4
♡ Q1052
◊ 96
♣ 97542
```

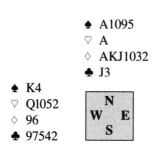

West	North	East	South
			1NT
Pass	2♣	Pass	2◊
Pass	4♣	Pass	4♡
Pass	7◊	All Pass	

After South opened a 13-15 point no-trump, North tried Stayman and then Gerber, South showing one ace.

You lead a trump and, having started with a doubleton Q8, South plays three rounds and seems likely to continue rattling off the suit. How do you plan your discards?

Solutions

Problem 2.1

You should realise that South may have a doubleton heart and it is likely that you will need to find partner with the ♡K to have a reasonable chance. That will leave South with the ♠AK for his Acol-style two-opener and you must consider the club position. You will also need to find partner with the ♣Q or to have a chance. The critical layout is one like this:

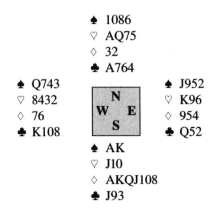

```
                    ♠ 1086
                    ♡ AQ75
                    ◊ 32
                    ♣ A764
  ♠ Q743                        ♠ J952
  ♡ 8432          N             ♡ K96
  ◊ 76          W   E           ◊ 954
  ♣ K108          S             ♣ Q52
                    ♠ AK
                    ♡ J10
                    ◊ AKQJ108
                    ♣ J93
```

You must keep your heart holding intact and throw another spade (or even a club). True, declarer could easily have the ♠AKJ and only two clubs, but he may still later take a finesse in spades. You will have two further discards to make, but by then you will have received a helpful discard from partner. Here, partner can discard the ♠9, showing you four cards in the suit (and tending to confirm the heart layout, since he should discard a low heart from three small) allowing you to discard all your spades on declarer's remaining diamonds. When declarer takes the heart finesse, East can win the first heart and return a club, preventing declarer from untangling his three heart winners, the position being:

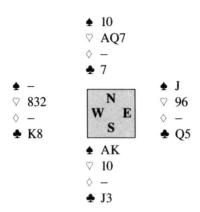

```
              ♠ 10
              ♡ AQ7
              ◇ –
              ♣ 7
♠ –                        ♠ J
♡ 832        ┌─────┐       ♡ 96
◇ –          │  N  │       ◇ –
♣ K8         │ W E │       ♣ Q5
             │  S  │
             └─────┘
              ♠ AK
              ♡ 10
              ◇ –
              ♣ J3
```

Partner's ♣Q prevents you from being squeezed.

Problem 2.2

Partner has obviously led from something like ♠A109xx and only one further lead from you will be necessary. You can thus easily afford one spade, but how about the other two discards, which will have to be red? When this came up, I was South and was presented with the contract when East threw two diamonds without giving the matter much thought:

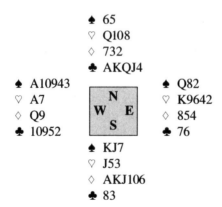

```
                ♠ 65
                ♡ Q108
                ◇ 732
                ♣ AKQJ4
♠ A10943                      ♠ Q82
♡ A7         ┌─────┐          ♡ K9642
◇ Q9         │  N  │          ◇ 854
♣ 10952      │ W E │          ♣ 76
             │  S  │
             └─────┘
                ♠ KJ7
                ♡ J53
                ◇ AKJ106
                ♣ 83
```

The crucial point was to consider what was going to happen after the clubs had been cashed. That would give declarer six tricks and if he had a strong heart holding over East's king, there was nothing to be done. The critical case arose when South was strong in diamonds, in particular in the layout above where declarer was saved a guess. It can hardly cost to throw three low hearts and hang on to those low diamonds, giving the impression of something worth holding in the suit. Declarer is now likely to get it wrong. Technically speaking, South might have tried one high diamond before cashing the clubs, protecting against a singleton ◊Q with East, but, as declarer at the time, I rejected that line as it would have made it all too obvious what my problem was.

We can now lay down another important tip:

Guiding Principle

When a long suit is being cashed against you and you are in difficulty with discards, the overriding consideration is the anticipation of what declarer is going to do afterwards.

Problem 2.3

A careful roll-call will keep you on the right track here. South is known to hold four diamonds and no four-card major so he has three or four clubs. West has shown the ◊QJ, three points and, with eleven in yours and nine in dummy, twenty-three points are so far accounted for. South will have sixteen or seventeen, but all the jacks are accounted for, the ◊J with West and the rest on view, so South has all remaining high cards. Now we shall count tricks. South cannot be denied three club tricks, two top spades and two top hearts to make seven so far. If he has a third heart, a finesse will give him an eighth. It is important not to give him a ninth by discarding a heart or a club and you will have to hope that partner has the ♠10 or, if he has not, that the deal looks like this:

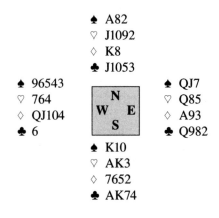

```
              ♠ A82
              ♡ J1092
              ◊ K8
              ♣ J1053
♠ 96543                        ♠ QJ7
♡ 764          N               ♡ Q85
◊ QJ104      W   E             ◊ A93
♣ 6            S               ♣ Q982
              ♠ K10
              ♡ AK3
              ◊ 7652
              ♣ AK74
```

South can use his only entry to dummy to take finesses in both clubs and hearts but, as long as you do not cover on the first round of either, you will ensure a fifth trick for your side.

An instructive footnote here is that it is very often wrong for the defenders to cash four tricks early, particularly in this kind of position where the bulk of strength is in one hand. That hand is almost certain to have discard problems later in the play. Here, if West switches to spades after three rounds of diamonds, the contract is still defeated.

Problem 2.4

You should have noticed a number of things. Firstly, regarding the play to trick one, partner is likely to give count in these situations, yet the ◊3 did not appear. Thus at this stage, you do not know the count of the diamonds with certainty. However, when East plays the ◊5 as his discard, it is probable that he is confirming an odd number and that South has concealed the ◊3 in an attempt to throw you off the rails. Secondly, partner's ♡10 probably came from queen, ten and others. If South has the ♡Q, he has four heart tricks, four clubs, three diamonds and, with any spade honour well-placed for him, will surely make the contract. Thus East must be credited with the ♡Q, leaving South with at least AKQ in spades. Now he has four club tricks, three spades, two hearts and three diamonds for twelve so far, implying that partner must have the ♠J for the defenders to have a chance. Looking at those spades in more detail on that assumption, you observe that, on the bidding, East is restricted to three spades and thus your only hope lies with that ♠8, implying that this must be the deal:

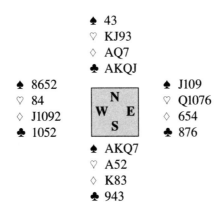

```
                      ♠ 43
                      ♡ KJ93
                      ◊ AQ7
                      ♣ AKQJ
        ♠ 8652                      ♠ J109
        ♡ 84          N             ♡ Q1076
        ◊ J1092     W   E           ◊ 654
        ♣ 1052        S             ♣ 876
                      ♠ AKQ7
                      ♡ A52
                      ◊ K83
                      ♣ 943
```

At all costs, therefore, you must keep parity with South in spades. You can discard your heart if you are in doubt about diamonds, but if you do, you will be showing out on the next heart, telling South that the finesse is wrong and you must now discard a diamond. Either defence will beat the contract, but it is very often wise to keep that heart in this kind of position on the basis that two rounds of hearts will definitely be played; it is not certain that there will be four rounds of diamonds. South might well take the finesse at once.

Problem 2.5

You first should have noticed the size of partner's clubs. Clearly he has led from something like ♣QJ108x and he chose the lowest cards he could afford. That suggests a preference for diamonds. But even without that, with opponents having announced four-card major suits, it is your first priority to keep parity with them. At best, partner can have two spades and three hearts and is unlikely to be able to help, at least lengthwise, in either although he may have a picture or two. In diamonds, however, there is every chance that partner has something significant. You should, therefore, have no qualms about endangering your queen and should discard from that suit:

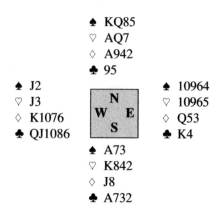

```
              ♠ KQ85
              ♡ AQ7
              ◊ A942
              ♣ 95
 ♠ J2                        ♠ 10964
 ♡ J3         ┌─────────┐    ♡ 10965
 ◊ K1076      │   N     │    ◊ Q53
 ♣ QJ1086     │ W     E │    ♣ K4
              │   S     │
              └─────────┘
              ♠ A73
              ♡ K842
              ◊ J8
              ♣ A732
```

As you see, partner has some help in the majors, honour-wise, and, provided you kept parity, your tens are promoted.

From these last two problems, we can lay down another tip.

Guiding Principle

When in difficulties with discarding, try to discard from the suit in which partner is likely to have length which is greater or equal to yours, i.e. where he is most likely to be able to help.

Problem 2.6

This is simply a matter of counting points. There are twenty-four in dummy and three in your hand to total twenty-seven so far. This implies that, even if South started with a minimum twelve, the best you can hope for is one point from partner, the only useful card being the ♠J. Provided it is guarded by two low cards, you can safely discard two spades so that you can keep parity with dummy's hearts:

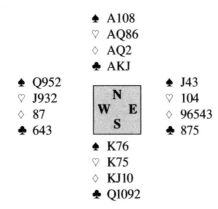

	♠ A108	
	♡ AQ86	
	◇ AQ2	
	♣ AKJ	
♠ Q952		♠ J43
♡ J932	**N**	♡ 104
◇ 87	**W E**	◇ 96543
♣ 643	**S**	♣ 875
	♠ K76	
	♡ K75	
	◇ KJ10	
	♣ Q1092	

As a matter of interest, even if South has the ♠J, implying that you were genuinely in trouble, it is still correct to throw spades, leaving South the option to finesse in the wrong direction. If you throw a heart, there is no chance. Declarer simply cashes from the top.

Problem 2.7

You have little problem with four discards; it is unlikely that you are going to get rich on hearts. So your four hearts can go, but what is going to happen when declarer then cashes the ♡A? You will be down to ♠Kx and your five little clubs. The bidding and early play indicates that South started with 3325 and you must watch his discards. If he hangs on to his clubs, so must you, even if it means blanking the ♠K, i.e. playing partner for at least the ♠J:

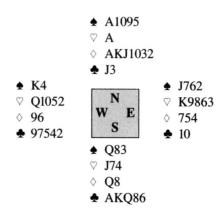

```
            ♠ A1095
            ♡ A
            ◇ AKJ1032
            ♣ J3
 ♠ K4                        ♠ J762
 ♡ Q1052      N             ♡ K9863
 ◇ 96      W     E          ◇ 754
 ♣ 97542      S             ♣ 10
            ♠ Q83
            ♡ J74
            ◇ Q8
            ♣ AKQ86
```

The bidding by North was optimistic, to say the least, but the contract was an excellent one, unluckily failing on the 5-1 club split and then only on correct defence.

These examples should be sufficient to emphasise the importance of recognising parity situations and keeping parity where it applies.

We now turn to situations in which declarer may benefit from the information available from our discards and we shall learn how to keep this to a minimum.

Chapter 3

Concealment

In this chapter, we shall be considering how the declarer can interpret information from defenders' discards and consequently learn how the defenders should discard to give away as little information away as possible. The first step will be to list a number of important commonly-occurring suit lay-outs and decide when it is and is not safe to discard.

As an example, we take the diamond suit, defending against a no-trump contract. Firstly, giving declarer three of the top four honours:

◇ AKQ6

◇ J852   ◇ 10973

◇ 4

Here either defender can discard as many as he likes provided the other keeps his full holding intact. But strengthen declarer's holding to:

◇ AKQ9

◇ J852   ◇ 10763

◇ 4

and now West can discard as he wishes if East holds on to everything while, if West is the one to keep his whole suit, East can only afford to discard three times; otherwise he exposes his partner to a first-round finesse.

Once we reduce declarer to:

◇ AKJ6

◇ 10852   ◇ Q973

◇ 4

West can discard everything while East should keep hold of all four cards, otherwise, if South reads the position correctly, he can drop the ◇Q to make three tricks instead of his initial entitlement of two. Placing the ◇Q with West:

◊ AKJ6

◊ Q1082   ◊ 9753

◊ 4

South is good for three tricks now if he reads the position correctly and takes the finesse. In that case, West can throw his entire suit if East keeps his intact or vice versa.

Where the defenders have the ◊K, South's length becomes more relevant:

◊ AQJ6

◊ K852   ◊ 10973

◊ 4

Here West must hold all four to restrict South to two tricks and East can do what he likes.

◊ AQJ9

◊ K85   ◊ 10762

◊ 43

Now nothing can prevent South taking three tricks and West can throw his whole suit if East keeps all his intact. It may be important for West to keep all three if South can only lead from his hand once. Now after the finesse and the ◊A, he will have to guess whether to play the ◊9 on the third round, catering for the above lie, or the ◊J catering for:

◊ AQJ9

◊ K852   ◊ 1076

◊ 43

Where declarer has only two honours, things can be become very complicated:

◊ A8

◊ J952   ◊ Q1076

◊ K43

Here either side can throw all four cards provided the other keeps three intact, but change to:

◇ A9

◇ J852   ◇ Q1076

◇ K43

Now East must keep his ◇Q to protect this partner for a first-round finesse. If East keeps at least three cards, West can throw everything.

◇ A1082

◇ J96   ◇ Q75

◇ K43

South is good for three tricks anyway. Either defender can throw one card but not more, otherwise he exposes his partner to a second-round finesse. The other defender must keep all three cards.

◇ A1082

◇ J975   ◇ Q6

◇ K43

Here again, South is good for three tricks, but East must not discard at all otherwise he exposes his partner to two finesses after the ◇K drops the ◇Q. West can afford one card.

Defenders must also be vigilant when declarer is on a guess. Often discarding from an honour may sway him the wrong way:

◇ Q982

◇ A76   ◇ J54

◇ K103

South needs to find the ◇J and note that East loses nothing if he discards one card. If South was going to finesse against him, the ◇J was dead anyway. If he was going to finesse against West on the second round, the ◇J will score anyway. What invariably happens in these situations is that East hangs on furiously to 'give his honour as much protection as possible' while West, not needing to protect his ace, discards, giving the position away. Defenders should, if anything, arrange for East to discard. We saw in a earlier chapter a position, (actually in clubs) which was something like:

◇ KJ8

◇ A965   ◇ Q107

◇ 432

East was under pressure to discard and proved reluctant to blank his queen. It costs nothing. West can come down to a doubleton and still give declarer a guess. However, West is best advised to keep three cards if possible; otherwise a correct guess will give South two tricks in the suit instead of his initial entitlement of one.

Once we get into suit contracts, the possibility of a suit being ruffed high comes into the reckoning and matters are complicated further. We could go on for hours, but this is a position in which the defenders regularly help declarer. Suppose that diamonds are a side suit in a spade contract:

$$\diamond \text{ AQ873}$$
$$\diamond \text{ 9654} \qquad\qquad \diamond \text{ KJ2}$$
$$\diamond \text{ 10}$$

West has to make an early discard and it is almost invariably wrong to throw a diamond. If South needs to bring the suit in, given no other information, he might well decide to take a finesse. On seeing the discard, he might prefer to take the view that West has no interest and try to ruff the suit out, making one extra trick.

Generally speaking, defenders will discard from long suits in which it is obvious that their long cards will not be needed. One of our top bridge writers, in a book on declarer play, rightly emphasised that declarer should take this into account and, more often than not, for example, a discard on an early round of trumps will indicate a five-card or longer holding. 4441 hands are always possible, but are relatively rare.

This is an example in which a declarer took advantage of this tip. Take the East seat:

Love All. Dealer West.

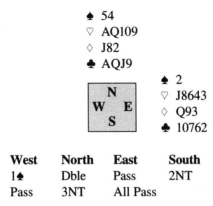

♠ 54
♡ AQ109
◇ J82
♣ AQJ9

♠ 2
♡ J8643
◇ Q93
♣ 10762

West	North	East	South
1♠	Dble	Pass	2NT
Pass	3NT	All Pass	

West leads the ♣K, which holds, South playing the ♣3. On the ♠10, indicating solid spades, you have to find a discard. What is it? This hand illustrates a useful point about card-reading:

Guiding principle

When placing outstanding honours from the East position and one or more tenace positions appear in dummy, clubs and hearts being the cases in point here, it will often be right to be optimistic by placing the finessable card(s) with declarer.

The ♣K and the ♡K are the crucial examples here. If West has them both, South should have the two top diamonds, and thus is cold for one spade trick, three clubs, two diamonds and three hearts, thus making the contract in comfort as West can never get in. However, try giving the two kings to South and then place the diamond honours. Clearly they will be split and the ◇A will have to be with West to justify the opening bid. That leaves the ◇K with South for thirteen points and a reasonable 2NT answer to the double.

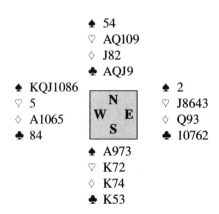

          ♠ 54
          ♡ AQ109
          ◇ J82
          ♣ AQJ9

♠ KQJ1086   ♠ 2
♡ 5   N   ♡ J8643
◇ A1065   W   E   ◇ Q93
♣ 84   S   ♣ 10762

          ♠ A973
          ♡ K72
          ◇ K74
          ♣ K53

So now it would appear that any discard is safe, but not if you are up against an eagle-eyed declarer. He will be looking to the heart suit as a source of tricks and, if you discard the 'useless' fifth heart, as is usually safe, he might roll-call the suit accurately. This is what happened at the table when the hand appeared many years ago. East discarded a heart and South cashed the ♡A and ran the ♡10 successfully to complete four tricks in the suit to go with four clubs and the ♠A. East could have discarded from either minor with impunity; a diamond is probably preferable to a club in that four rounds of clubs are likely to be played and you will save a trick when West does have the ♣K and the ◇K when the defenders still have a chance. It is less certain that a diamond discard will cost.

So we can lay down a further tip:

Guiding Principle

If it is clear that a suit will be played, the less you tell declarer the better, even if the discard, considered in isolation, does not appear to cost.

On the above hand, declarer may draw (possibly correct) conclusions if you do not discard a heart. It could also be argued that you should discard a heart from some holding like ♡xxx on the grounds that declarer will now play you for ♡Jxxxx and finesse his way to defeat with the suit breaking evenly all the time. But that is all another matter. Experience shows that the less said the better; avoid discarding from either holding.

With that borne in mind, try the following examples; attempt to anticipate which suits are likely to be played and think twice before the making the automatic choice of a 'useless long suit'.

Quiz on Concealment

Problem 3.1
Love All. Dealer East.

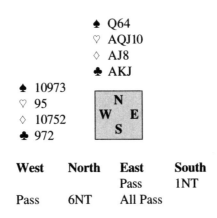

```
              ♠ Q64
              ♡ AQJ10
              ◇ AJ8
              ♣ AKJ
  ♠ 10973
  ♡ 95           N
  ◇ 10752     W     E
  ♣ 972          S
```

West	North	East	South
		Pass	1NT
Pass	6NT	All Pass	

South's opener promised 12-14 points.

You lead the ♠10 and dummy's ♠Q is played. Partner wins with the ♠A, South playing the ♠2, and returns the ♠8, won by South's ♠K. The ♡K follows and declarer continues the suit, discarding the ♣3 on the third round. Partner following with ♡4, ♡6, ♡2 – a curious sequence that seems to indicate that he does not wish to give a clear signal. How do you discard?

Problem 3.2
North/South Game. Dealer East.

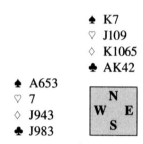

♠ K7
♡ J109
◇ K1065
♣ AK42

♠ A653
♡ 7
◇ J943
♣ J983

West	North	East	South
		Pass	1♡
Pass	2♣	Pass	3♡
Pass	4NT	Pass	5♣
Pass	6♡	All Pass	

North's 4NT was Roman Key-card Blackwood, South responding to show 0 or 3 (here obviously 3) key cards, i.e. aces and the king of trumps.

Reluctant to touch a side suit, you decide to lead your trump and declarer takes three rounds, overtaking on the third while partner follows with the ♡5, ♡6 and ♡8. You can easily spare two low spades on tricks two and three, but how do you propose to discard on any further rounds of trumps?

Problem 3.3
East/West Game. Dealer West.

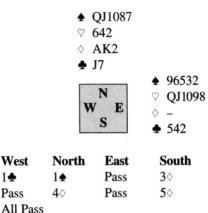

♠ QJ1087
♡ 642
◇ AK2
♣ J7

♠ 96532
♡ QJ1098
◇ –
♣ 542

West	North	East	South
1♣	1♠	Pass	3◇
Pass	4◇	Pass	5◇
All Pass			

East/West were playing a five-card major-suit style so the opening bid guaranteed three or more clubs.

Partner leads the two top clubs and you follow with ♣2 and ♣4 and declarer with the ♣9 and ♣10. Partner now switches to the ◇8 and dummy plays low. What do you discard?

Problem 3.4
Love All. Dealer East.

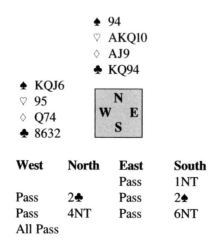

```
              ♠ 94
              ♡ AKQ10
              ◇ AJ9
              ♣ KQ94
  ♠ KQJ6
  ♡ 95            N
  ◇ Q74       W      E
  ♣ 8632          S
```

West	North	East	South
		Pass	1NT
Pass	2♣	Pass	2♠
Pass	4NT	Pass	6NT
All Pass			

A 12-14 point opener was followed by Stayman and the partnership played North's 4NT as quantitative.

You lead the ♠K and South's ♠A wins as partner follows with the ♠3 . South starts cashing the hearts. How do you plan to discard?

Solutions

Problem 3.1

Your first duty is to roll-call the hand as far as possible. Declarer has promised at least twelve points and twenty-two have been tabled, leaving at most six for partner including the ♠A already played. The best you can hope for is a minor-suit queen. The next job is to roll-call the spade suit. If partner's ♠A was doubleton, leaving South with four and you with a potential stop, declarer could have ducked in dummy at trick one and led a low spade from there later, dropping partner's ♠A on air and making a probably crucial third trick in the suit. It is therefore reasonable to assume that South has three spades and that you can discard spades with impunity:

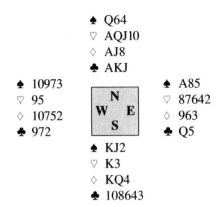

```
                        ♠ Q64
                        ♡ AQJ10
                        ◇ AJ8
                        ♣ AKJ
      ♠ 10973                         ♠ A85
      ♡ 95          ┌─────────┐       ♡ 87642
      ◇ 10752       │   N     │       ◇ 963
      ♣ 972         │ W   E   │       ♣ Q5
                    │   S     │
                    └─────────┘
                        ♠ KJ2
                        ♡ K3
                        ◇ KQ4
                        ♣ 108643
```

Observe that a club discard could be fatal, swaying declarer from the odds-on finesse to the drop. It is clear that, if declarer has the ♣Q, at least three rounds of the suit will be played and you might as well hold your three cards in the suit anyway. After the hearts, you will have to discard a diamond if declarer plays his third spade, but your spades should be the first cards to go.

It is worth commenting that South might well have played low from dummy at trick one, but his idea was to force the ♠A out as soon as possible to tighten the position to maximum effect, hoping that you will discard a 'useless' club if the ♣Q is doubleton offside. If he ducks the spade at trick one, East might well do the same and refuse even a second round. South cannot now risk a third round as East might have started with ♠Axxx. Defenders' discards are now that much easier. East does better play low at trick one anyway.

I have gone into some detail on this matter as it will become critical when we discuss squeeze-play defence later on.

Problem 3.2

Clearly you are in some difficulties, as either minor suit may be coming in if you discard from it. You should have realised a number of points. You can count declarer for six heart tricks, two top diamonds and two top clubs to total ten so far. If he has the spade queen, that brings the total to eleven. If he has *three* spades to the queen, he would have arranged to ruff a spade in dummy, so we can rule that out. However, even if declarer has only one or two spades the position is hopeless because that would give declarer at least five minor-suit cards. Regardless of how they are located, we will inevitably be squeezed in the minors.

The critical case is more likely to arise when partner has the ♠Q and declarer one of the minor-suit queens. You have to hope that declarer has ♠J10 in which case he may have a guess and you must keep the losing option open by retaining a low card with your ♠A.

Even now, your problems are far from over, since you are going to be subjected to considerable pressure in the minors. Since you need some help from partner in the minors, you must assume that South has only four minor-suit cards. The critical cases are: ◊AQx ♣x; ◊Axx ♣Q; ◊A ♣Qxx and ◊AQ ♣xx (if South has ◊Ax ♣Qx again you will be squeezed). In the first and fourth cases only a club discard will keep you alive, but in the third case you need to discard diamonds. Today is your lucky day, since the full hand is:

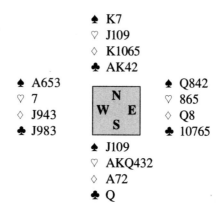

                          ♠ K7
                          ♡ J109
                          ◊ K1065
                          ♣ AK42
    ♠ A653   ♠ Q842
    ♡ 7   N   ♡ 865
    ◊ J943   W   E   ◊ Q8
    ♣ J983   S   ♣ 10765
                          ♠ J109
                          ♡ AKQ432
                          ◊ A72
                          ♣ Q

On this lie, you can actually discard from either minor without ruining the defence. The important point is that you kept two spades and you can take full credit even if you discarded a diamond as opposed to the technically superior club.

Now, if dummy throws a minor-suit card, you will be safe to throw a similar card on the next trump and dummy will be forced to discard again. Declarer can keep the position hot be throwing a second diamond as he still has a threat in his hand, but the defenders can survive even a sixth round of trumps, West keeping two spades, three diamonds and two clubs and East one spade, two diamonds and four clubs. Eventually, South is going to have to guess the spade position. If East has smoothly blanked his ♠Q, the chances are that South will get it wrong.

Let's get back to that position discussed earlier where South has the ♠Q doubleton and East both minor-suit queens:

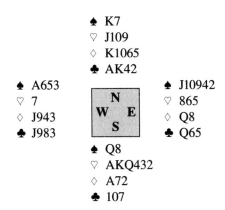

♠ K7
♡ J109
◇ K1065
♣ AK42

♠ A653
♡ 7
◇ J943
♣ J983

♠ J10942
♡ 865
◇ Q8
♣ Q65

♠ Q8
♡ AKQ432
◇ A72
♣ 107

When South runs five rounds of hearts, an early discard of a club will allow him to set up a trick in that suit by ruffing, so you must discard three spades and a diamond, while dummy discards two diamonds. You will now be given the ♠A, dummy unblocking, and will have to return a minor. Declarer wins, completes three rounds of clubs, ruffing in hand with his last trump and now the ♠K squeezes you in the minors.

Problem 3.3

A signalling 'expert' will be quick to tell you that the ♡Q would be a highly informative discard, promising solid cards behind the queen while denying the king. Highly informative, yes – but to declarer! The ♡Q is all right in the context of heart suit itself, but not in the context of the whole hand.

Can you envisage declarer's problem? He has already lost two club tricks and must take the rest. That implies that he must have the ♠A and, if he has the ♠K as well, the hand is over unless partner has four trumps. In that case the defence will not matter; declarer has no chance with 2362. The critical case arises when declarer is 1372 with potential to bring the spade suit in as here:

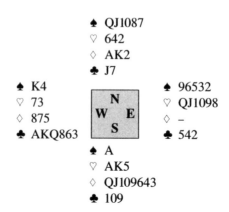

♠ QJ1087
♡ 642
◇ AK2
♣ J7

♠ K4
♡ 73
◇ 875
♣ AKQ863

♠ 96532
♡ QJ1098
◇ –
♣ 542

♠ A
♡ AK5
◇ QJ109643
♣ 109

When declarer is 2272 he needs to find the ♠K. In either case, if you discard the ♡Q, you advertise the position of the ♡J and announce to declarer that his only hope is to drop the ♠K rather than take a ruffing finesse against your hand. (He will roll-call the points and realise that, if you have the ♠K, partner has opened on nine points and you did not answer on six and side-suit void – not really on!) You should therefore refrain from advertising the heart position, either by discarding your last club or, probably best, a low heart.

Now, restricted to two entries to dummy, declarer must decide whether partner has the ♠K, in which case the drop is the only hope, or that he has opened on three top clubs and one or both heart honours and you have the ♠K. For that reason, I recommend not discarding a spade. That might give the impression that you are not interested in the suit and are holding a heart honour – strong evidence that the ♠K is with West.

Declarer may still get it right anyway, but discarding the ♡Q is a certain way to point him in the right direction.

Problem 3.4

You can do a very accurate roll-call on this hand. Nineteen points are on view in dummy and you have eight yourself, so you can place all the outstanding honours with South. Declarer must have eleven top tricks: one spade, four hearts, two diamonds and four clubs, and the diamond finesse could give him twelve. The crucial card is the ◇10. If South does not hold it, there is only one way he can take the diamond finesse and your ◇Q has no hope. So you must credit the ◇10 to South and he now has a choice.

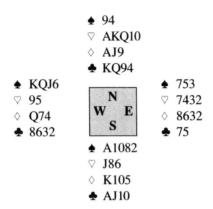

South will cash four tricks in both clubs and hearts. He has already taken the ♠A, so you will have to come down to four cards. What will South hold? Probably one spade and three diamonds:

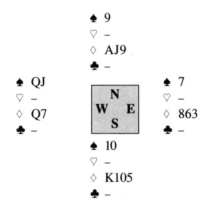

If you prefer to keep one spade and three diamonds, you will be thrown in with your spade winner, saving declarer the diamond guess. In this kind of situation, it pays not to leave the painful diamond discard to the last moment, but to do it now, on the third heart, giving declarer the impression that you have no interest in that quarter. East, with his dazzling hand, must play his part by hanging on to his three low diamonds like grim death to give declarer the maximum chance to go wrong.

We now turn to situations where we need recognise the need to discard winners or stops in suits because we know that declarer cannot reach them.

Chapter 4

Recognising the Unnecessary

Thousands of points are thrown to the winds daily through defenders grimly hanging on to 'no-hopers', cards which are masters in their suit, but which will never score because no further rounds of that suit will be played. The mistake is particularly inexcusable when the suit is in dummy and the defender can see the position clearly. Where the suit it is in declarer's hand, the position is admittedly more difficult and now the defender must ask himself whether declarer is strong enough to have a side-suit entry.

Guiding Principle

If it is clear that there is no way in which any further rounds of a particular suit will be played, it will usually be right to discard from that suit, be your cards winners or losers.

We shall look at a couple of simple examples, seeing all four hands:

North/South Game. Dealer North.

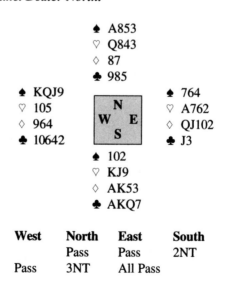

	♠ A853		
	♡ Q843		
	◇ 87		
	♣ 985		

West	North	East	South
	Pass	Pass	2NT
Pass	3NT	All Pass	

West started with the ♠K, which held, as did the ♠Q. Dummy won the third round, South discarding a diamond, and a heart followed to his ♡K, which won. A second heart was won by South's ♡J, West having petered to give count, and a third round went to East's ♡A, West discarding a diamond. East switched to the ◊Q, which was allowed to hold, but South won the second round and cashed a third round. At this point, West could see this:

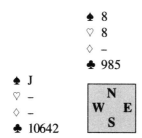

```
                    ♠ 8
                    ♡ 8
                    ◊ –
                    ♣ 985
        ♠ J
        ♡ –             ┌─────────┐
        ◊ –             │    N    │
        ♣ 10642         │  W   E  │
                        │    S    │
                        └─────────┘
```

With dummy's ♠8 'threatening', discarding his 'obvious' spade winner was more than West could bear, so he threw a club, presenting declarer with a fourth club trick and the contract. It seems so obvious that the ♠J will never score unless West can get in, and that could only be with clubs. It was therefore necessary to keep the club position as strong as possible and throw the spade winner. Remember that the defenders had already taken four tricks and only one more was needed. Yet the number of people who would throw a club in this, or similar positions, is staggering.

Observe that West could have foreseen the danger on a points roll-call. South had shown nothing in spades, the king and jack of hearts (four points), the ace and king of diamonds (another seven) to total eleven so far and thus he needed at least the top three clubs for twenty, the minimum for the 2NT opener. The only hope was to find partner with the ♣J.

For our second example, the 'threat' was not on view:

East/West Game. Dealer North.

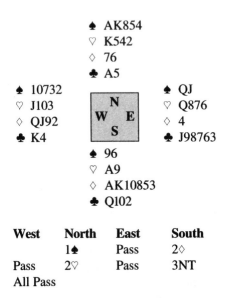

	♠ AK854	
	♡ K542	
	◊ 76	
	♣ A5	

♠ 10732		♠ QJ
♡ J103		♡ Q876
◊ QJ92		◊ 4
♣ K4		♣ J98763

	♠ 96	
	♡ A9	
	◊ AK10853	
	♣ Q102	

West	North	East	South
	1♠	Pass	2◊
Pass	2♡	Pass	3NT
All Pass			

West did well to find the ♡J as his lead and, to preserve the entry, declarer won immediately in dummy. A diamond followed, to the ◊10 and West's ◊J and a second heart was won perforce by South's ♡A. Now South tested the diamonds and had to cash both his tops or go without one of the tricks in that suit; dummy discarded a heart and East two low clubs. Declarer now ducked a spade round to East, who cashed his ♡Q, South discarding a club. On the fourth round of hearts, South discarded a diamond leaving:

	♠ AK85
	♡ –
	◊ –
	♣ A5

♠ 1073	
♡ –	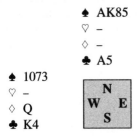
◊ Q	
♣ K4	

It seemed folly to blank the ♣K, and, with South threatening diamond winners, it looked right to hold the 'stopper' and discard a spade. Dummy discarded a club and South claimed the remainder. There was no point at all in West's holding on to that diamond when it was obvious that there was no way that South could get to his hand to cash his established winners. Meanwhile the spades were threatening and dummy had the benefit of the obvious entry. Yet again, the number of people who would have held on to that ◇Q is alarming.

Try the following examples, demonstrating that you can see where the danger lies and also where it does not lie.

Quiz on discarding 'winners'

Problem 4.1
East/West Game. Dealer North.

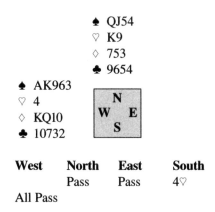

	♠ QJ54	
	♡ K9	
	◇ 753	
	♣ 9654	

West	North	East	South
	Pass	Pass	4♡
All Pass			

You lead the ♠A to the ♠4, ♠2 and ♠8. You try the ◇K and, when partner encourages with the ◇8, you continue, South producing the ◇J on the second and ruffing the third. Now follow five rounds of trumps; partner follows three times and then discards a spade. On the fifth, you can see:

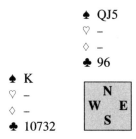

	♠ QJ5
	♡ –
	◇ –
	♣ 96

You know that South still has another trump to come. How do you defend?

Problem 4.2
North/South Game. Dealer South.

```
                    ♠ 85
                    ♡ J10987
                    ◊ A32
                    ♣ 964
                                  ♠ 109
              ┌─────────┐         ♡ AKQ63
              │    N    │         ◊ 754
              │ W     E │         ♣ QJ5
              │    S    │
              └─────────┘
```

West	North	East	South
			2♣
Pass	2◊	2♡	3♠
Pass	4◊	Pass	6♠
All Pass			

The 'unnecessary' jump to 3♠ in a game-forcing situation showed a solid
self-supporting suit and asked North to cue-bid.

West leads the ♡4 and your ♡Q is ruffed by South, who follows with six
rounds of trumps. West follows twice and then discards his remaining
hearts, one club and one diamond. You will have to find four discards – what
are they?

Problem 4.3
East/West Game. Dealer West.

♠ A754
♡ AK93
◊ 10
♣ KJ106

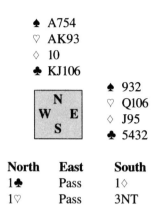

♠ 932
♡ Q106
◊ J95
♣ 5432

West	North	East	South
Pass	1♣	Pass	1◊
Pass	1♡	Pass	3NT
All Pass			

West leads the ♠Q, which runs to the ♠4, ♠2 and ♠K. South leads the ♣8 and West's ♣A wins, dummy following with the ♣10. West's ♠J is won in dummy, South following with the ♠6. The ◊10 is led; you cover and South's ◊Q loses to West's ◊K. West cashes two more spades, on which you throw a club, and South discards two low diamonds. Now the ♡8 is won in dummy with the ♡A as you encourage with the ♡10 and South drops the ♡J. Declarer crosses to hand by overtaking the ♣J with the ♣Q, partner discarding a low heart, and cashes the ◊A, dummy discarding a heart. Now comes the ♣9 to the ♣K, partner again discarding a low heart. On the ♡K, declarer discards a low diamond. That completes eleven tricks and you can now see:

♠ –
♡ 9
◊ –
♣ 6

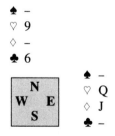

♠ –
♡ Q
◊ J
♣ –

Now declarer leads the ♣6 from dummy. What do you discard?

Problem 4.4
East/West Game. Dealer West.

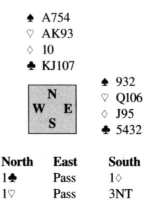

```
        ♠ A754
        ♡ AK93
        ◊ 10
        ♣ KJ107
                        ♠ 932
              N         ♡ Q106
          W     E       ◊ J95
              S         ♣ 5432
```

West	North	East	South
Pass	1♣	Pass	1◊
Pass	1♡	Pass	3NT
All Pass			

West leads the ♠Q, which runs to the ♠4, ♠2 and ♠K. South leads the ♣8 and West's ♣A wins, dummy following with the ♣10. West's ♠J is won in dummy, South following with the ♠6. Now the ◊10 is led; you cover and South's ◊Q loses to West's ◊K. West cashes two more spades, on which you throw a club and South discards two low diamonds. Now the ♡8 is won in dummy with the ♡A as you encourage with the ♡10 and South drops the ♡J. Declarer crosses to hand by overtaking the ♣J with the ♣Q, partner discarding a low heart, and cashes the ◊A, dummy discarding a heart. Now comes the ♣9 to the ♣K, partner again discarding a low heart. On the ♡K, declarer discards a low diamond. That completes eleven tricks and you can now see:

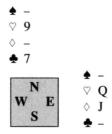

```
        ♠ –
        ♡ 9
        ◊ –
        ♣ 7
                        ♠ –
              N         ♡ Q
          W     E       ◊ J
              S         ♣ –
```

Declarer now leads the ♣7 from dummy. What do you discard?

Solutions

Problem 4.1

It was likely on the bidding, and confirmed by partner's encouragement of diamonds and his subsequent discarding, that South had one spade and partner three. Therefore declarer cannot reach those spades in dummy. You should discard your ♠K and one low club:

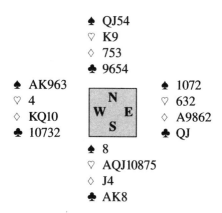

```
                    ♠ QJ54
                    ♡ K9
                    ◇ 753
                    ♣ 9654
    ♠ AK963                      ♠ 1072
    ♡ 4           ┌─────────┐    ♡ 632
    ◇ KQ10        │   N     │    ◇ A9862
    ♣ 10732       │ W   E   │    ♣ QJ
                  │   S     │
                  └─────────┘
                    ♠ 8
                    ♡ AQJ10875
                    ◇ J4
                    ♣ AK8
```

Discarding two clubs gives declarer the contract. You can see that the spades are no danger.

Problem 4.2

The crucial point to realise here is that, while declarer has an entry to ruff a further heart, even if that established the suit, he would have no further entry to cash the winners. Therefore, you should appreciate that it is only necessary to keep one top heart honour, no more. The very obvious temptation to discard the three low diamonds proves fatal in this type of lay-out:

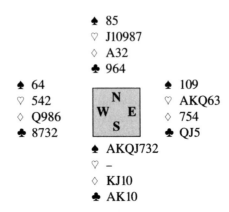

```
              ♠ 85
              ♡ J10987
              ◊ A32
              ♣ 964
♠ 64                          ♠ 109
♡ 542          N              ♡ AKQ63
◊ Q986     W       E          ◊ 754
♣ 8732         S              ♣ QJ5
              ♠ AKQJ732
              ♡ –
              ◊ KJ10
              ♣ AK10
```

South has now been told the position of the ◊Q and will finesse accordingly. You should keep your clubs, but should discard three hearts and only one diamond. Now each defender has discarded one diamond and South will be none the wiser. If anything, your discard of a 'precious' heart honour may well cause South to go wrong. Anyway, I have had countless successes through hanging on to low cards in critical suits in this kind of situation and even more as declarer through defenders giving away finesse positions.

Problem 4.3

You know that, as partner discarded on the second round of clubs, declarer started with four and that, as you had ♣5432, declarer's remaining club is higher than the ♣6. Thus his other card cannot be a heart and you must hang on to your diamond. The deal:

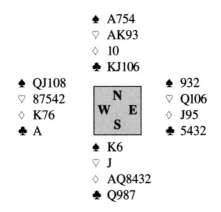

```
              ♠ A754
              ♡ AK93
              ◊ 10
              ♣ KJ106
♠ QJ108                       ♠ 932
♡ 87542        N              ♡ Q106
◊ K76      W       E          ◊ J95
♣ A            S              ♣ 5432
              ♠ K6
              ♡ J
              ◊ AQ8432
              ♣ Q987
```

Your ◊J will then beat South's ◊8.

Problem 4.4

This looks familiar and yet there has been a very subtle difference. Did you watch those club pips carefully enough? If you did, you will realise that South's last club is the ♣6 and thus that the ♣7 will hold this trick, leaving dummy on play. This time you must discard your ◊J and hold the ♡Q, to win the last trick. The deal:

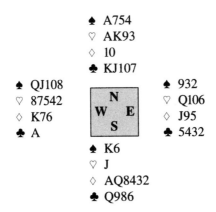

```
                    ♠ A754
                    ♡ AK93
                    ◊ 10
                    ♣ KJ107
   ♠ QJ108        ┌─────────┐        ♠ 932
   ♡ 87542        │    N    │        ♡ Q106
   ◊ K76          │  W   E  │        ◊ J95
   ♣ A            │    S    │        ♣ 5432
                  └─────────┘
                    ♠ K6
                    ♡ J
                    ◊ AQ8432
                    ♣ Q986
```

From these problems, the last two illustrating how careful you have to be, we can lay down are next tip:

Guiding Principle

When discarding under pressure in the endgame, it is crucial to know which opponent (i.e. declarer or dummy) is going to win each trick. If it is clear that a particular hand has no chance of getting in, you can safely discard from the suit in that hand, confident that no further rounds of it will be played.

So far, we have learnt how to discard accurately to keep our high-card winners intact. In the next chapter, as if there weren't enough problems, we are going to learn that, while it could be argued that, in real life, there is no such thing as being too rich, at the bridge table that does not necessarily apply. There are situations in which high cards can be a positive embarrassment and the sooner they are disposed of the better.

Chapter 5

Discarding to Unblock

Blockage problems for both declarer and defenders occur hand after hand and are best introduced with a few simple illustrations. Consider, as example, the heart suit as held by East/West in defence against a no-trump contract:

a)　　♡ A　　　　　　　♡ KQJ107

b)　　♡ K　　　　　　　♡ QJ1094

c)　　♡ Q　　　　　　　♡ J1096

In each case, we assume that East has no outside entries.

In a) we see that East has plenty of winners to cash, but West must win the first round and the East hand is now out of the game.

In b) the ♡A has been knocked out at an early stage; again West will win the first round and East has no further hope.

In c) both the ♡A and ♡K have been knocked out early in the play, but again, after West has won the first round, East can give up hope.

In all cases, how much better it would have been if West, instead of holding a stiff honour, were now holding a low card which he could lead to his partner's winners! The object of this chapter will be to learn to recognise positions where blockages are likely to occur and to throw your potentially offending honours away as soon as possible.

Many of these positions occur in no-trump contracts, but suit contracts are by no means exempt, as we shall see later. Very often a defender has to unblock in declarer's suit to ensure that his partner gets in to lead towards a tenace position. However, the commonest opportunities occur when East has made a bid and West leads his partner's suit against a no-trump contract. If, after one or two rounds, West has the opportunity to discard, he may be able to create an entry to his partner's hand by unblocking, notably in declarer's long suit.

To illustrate, let us assume a very common position where East has opened a weak 2♠, South has overcalled 2NT, and North has raised to 3NT. The spade position looks like this:

♠ 86

♠ 94   ♠ AQJ532

♠ K107

West leads the ♠9 and East puts on the ♠J. Now, if South wins immediately, East-West are still in communication in the suit and there is little further to discuss. Declarer will run home for nine tricks now or never. So South refuses trick one, keeping his stopper intact. But now East cashes his ♠A and plays a third round, giving West an opportunity to discard. South intends to make the contract by bringing in a long club suit in dummy so we shall now look at a number of everyday situations in that suit:

a)   ♣ AK9764   e)   ♣ AJ108642
   ♣ Q3   ♣ J52   ♣ K5   ♣ Q7
             ♣ 108   ♣ 93

b)   ♣ AK964   f)   ♣ KQ10753
   ♣ Q75   ♣ J82   ♣ A6   ♣ J92
             ♣ 103   ♣ 84

c)   ♣ AQ8642   g)   ♣ KJ108753
   ♣ K9   ♣ J53   ♣ A2   ♣ Q9
             ♣ 107   ♣ 64

d)   ♣ AQ862   h)   ♣ QJ108764
   ♣ K107   ♣ J53   ♣ A   ♣ K
             ♣ 94   ♣ 9532

Looking from declarer's point of view, we shall play each combination to establish the suit without letting East into the lead. In all cases, we observe the usual guide of leading from weakness through strength to strength, effectively forcing West to commit himself in front of North.

With a) and b) if West plays low on the first round, we win in dummy, return to South and try another low club. In a) the ♣Q will now appear and will be allowed to hold. In b) if West plays low again, dummy wins and now a third round clears the suit, again losing to West. If West chooses to play the ♣Q, dummy ducks and again the trick is lost to the non-dangerous hand.

With c) and d) the idea is similar. Play a low club from South. If West plays low, win as cheaply as possible, i.e. with the ♣Q, return to South in a red suit and repeat the exercise. When the ♣K appears, it is allowed to hold the trick.

With e) again South plays a low club; if West plays low, the ♣A is played and a second round ensures a loss to the ♣K with West. If West plays the ♣K on the first round, it is allowed to hold the trick.

With f) and g) it is a simple matter of leading towards the ♣K, twice in the first case, once in the second.

In h) any lead will suffice.

But now consider the effect if West has been able to discard his honour at an early stage.

We shall look at some examples with a full deal on view:

Game All. Dealer East.

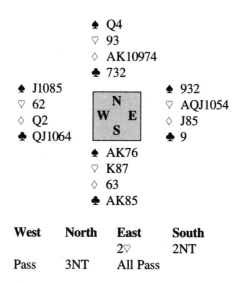

```
                    ♠ Q4
                    ♡ 93
                    ♦ AK10974
                    ♣ 732
    ♠ J1085                        ♠ 932
    ♡ 62          N                ♡ AQJ1054
    ♦ Q2       W     E             ♦ J85
    ♣ QJ1064      S                ♣ 9
                    ♠ AK76
                    ♡ K87
                    ♦ 63
                    ♣ AK85
```

West	North	East	South
		2♡	2NT
Pass	3NT	All Pass	

West led the ♡6 and East's ♡10 held. East continued with the ♡A and then the ♡J, forcing South to win. Now West faced the critical point of the defence. If he fails to discard the ♦Q, South plays a diamond towards dummy and then returns to hand in clubs to play another diamond towards dummy. When the ♦Q is played, she is allowed to hold the trick. The ♠Q acts as entry and South makes a comfortable five diamond tricks, three spades, two clubs and the heart for (apparently) eleven tricks, but actually only ten as he has conceded two hearts and the diamond. But now assume that West drops the ♦Q on the third round of hearts. South is now held to the heart, three spades, two clubs and two diamonds for eight tricks only.

A similar approach is needed here:

Love All. Dealer East.

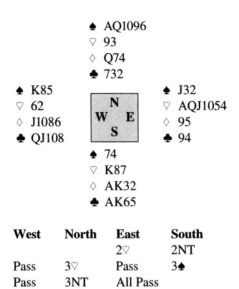

```
              ♠ AQ1096
              ♡ 93
              ◊ Q74
              ♣ 732
   ♠ K85                      ♠ J32
   ♡ 62          N            ♡ AQJ1054
   ◊ J1086    W   E           ◊ 95
   ♣ QJ108       S            ♣ 94
              ♠ 74
              ♡ K87
              ◊ AK32
              ♣ AK65
```

West	North	East	South
		2♡	2NT
Pass	3♡	Pass	3♠
Pass	3NT	All Pass	

Here North, by the transfer sequence, showed a five-card spade suit and an otherwise balanced hand, offering the alternative games of 3NT or 4♠, according to South's attitude to spades.

Again, West led the ♡6, East's ♡10 winning. Now the ♡A was followed by the ♡Q and West had to find a discard. Only the ♠K defeats the contract. If West holds on to that card, South plays a spade to the ♠Q, returns to the South hand in either minor and leads another spade. If West plays low again, dummy rises with the ♠A and a third round clears the suit in safety. If West plays the ♠K on either the first of second rounds of the suit, he is allowed to hold and again the rest of the suit can be cashed without East gaining the lead.

But if West has disembarrassed himself of the ♠K on the third heart, East is in control and South is held to eight tricks.

The same idea is applicable on the next deal:

North/South Game. Dealer East.

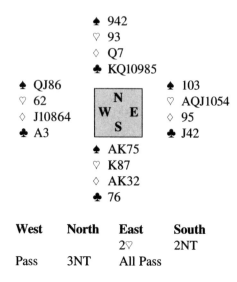

```
              ♠ 942
              ♡ 93
              ♢ Q7
              ♣ KQ10985
♠ QJ86                        ♠ 103
♡ 62          ┌──────┐        ♡ AQJ1054
♢ J10864      │  N   │        ♢ 95
♣ A3          │ W  E │        ♣ J42
              │  S   │
              └──────┘
              ♠ AK75
              ♡ K87
              ♢ AK32
              ♣ 76
```

West	North	East	South
		2♡	2NT
Pass	3NT	All Pass	

Again West led the ♡6 and East's ♡10 held. Now the ♡A was followed by the ♡4 and South had to win, leaving West with a discard. He has to realise that South will have to bring in those clubs to have any chance at all and that he will succeed by leading twice towards dummy, losing a trick to the harmless hand. Unless, that is, West gets rid of that ♣A quickly, playing his partner for a club stop in ♣Jxx.

What's this? Discarding aces? Didn't an American, a Mr. Bennett, in 1931 get an early bath for a lot less than that? This kind of defence seems unthinkable to the average player. But if you look at the club position carefully, converting from:

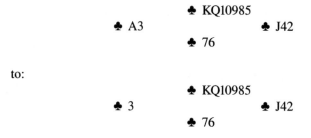

```
              ♣ KQ10985
♣ A3                         ♣ J42
              ♣ 76
```

to:

```
              ♣ KQ10985
♣ 3                          ♣ J42
              ♣ 76
```

It has meant no more than changing from five tricks won by declarer and one by the defenders to exactly the same score with the subtle difference that the defenders' trick will be won by East rather than West; but that is all the difference in the world. The defenders take five tricks instead of three.

But, of course, one question remains unanswered and this will be a very meticulous test of your reading habits and how much attention you pay to detail. How does West know that this kind of spectacular unblock is required? It could be completely wrong, and worse still, West will look incredibly stupid if he chucks the contract with such a discard. For example, in the second of the above hands, the spade situation was actually:

♠ AQ1096

♠ K85   ♠ J32

♠ 74

It could just as easily have been:

♠ AQ1096

♠ K85   ♠ J3

♠ 742

No – that does not mean that South would have preferred 4♠. He would have still stuck to 3NT with 3343 or 3334. Now, in this lower layout, the defenders have one trick in the suit if West holds his ♠K, but none if he discards it and there may be other ways to defeat the contract.

Well, did you notice subtle differences in the way the three hands were defended, in particular which heart was chosen by East for trick three? In the first, it was the ♡J, a middling card (he was still holding the ♡Q and lower cards); in the second it was his highest card, the ♡Q; in the third it was his lowest card, the ♡4. The choice of card in these situations (i.e. where it does not matter for the heart suit itself) should show suit preference with the other three suits being the candidates, a middle card for diamonds, a high card for spades, a low card for clubs. If East does not indicate his entry in dummy's long suit, the spectacular unblock card should be ruled out and West should seek other ways to beat the contract.

We can emphasise this point as a general tip:

Guiding Principle

When defenders are knocking out declarer's stop(s) in a suit and the card played does not matter in the context of defenders' long suit, the opportunity should be taken to show suit preference.

As we saw in the three model examples, South is going to be obliged to play his ♡K on the third round of the suit, irrespective of which card East chooses so East can indicate suit preference to his partner with his choice of card.

Having seen the idea, I should like you to do the following problems, stating your discard and justifying it as usual.

Quiz on unblocking

Problem 5.1
North/South Game. Dealer North.

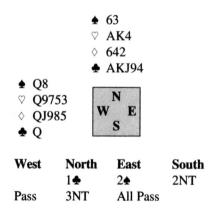

```
                      ♠ 63
                      ♡ AK4
                      ◇ 642
                      ♣ AKJ94
   ♠ Q8              ┌───────┐
   ♡ Q9753           │   N   │
   ◇ QJ985           │ W   E │
   ♣ Q               │   S   │
                     └───────┘
```

West	North	East	South
	1♣	2♠	2NT
Pass	3NT	All Pass	

You lead the ♠Q and it holds, as partner encourages with the ♠9. On the next round, partner wins with the ♠A and continues with the ♠2. South wins with the ♠K. What do you discard? Have you any further comment?

Problem 5.2
Love All. Dealer South.

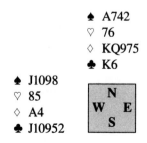

```
                      ♠ A742
                      ♡ 76
                      ◇ KQ975
                      ♣ K6
   ♠ J1098           ┌───────┐
   ♡ 85              │   N   │
   ◇ A4              │ W   E │
   ♣ J10952          │   S   │
                     └───────┘
```

West	North	East	South
			1NT
Pass	2♣	2♡	Pass
Pass	3♡	Pass	3NT
All Pass			

Note that a double of 3♡ by East in this type of sequence only helps the opponents. Now a pass from South would indicate no stop, a redouble a half-stop and 3NT a full stop. Opponents have far more room for accurate bidding. West should not need to be told twice to lead the suit!

You lead the ♡8 to the ♡6, ♡10 and ♡2. Now follows partner's ♡A and ♡J, South winning with the ♡K. What do you discard?

Problem 5.3
Love All. Dealer East.

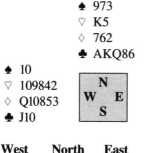

    ♠ 973
    ♡ K5
    ◇ 762
    ♣ AKQ86

♠ 10
♡ 109842
◇ Q10853
♣ J10

West	North	East	South
		1♠	Pass
Pass	2♣	Pass	2NT
Pass	3NT	All Pass	

You lead your ♠10 and partner wins with the ♠K, follows with the ♠A and then plays the ♠2, South's ♠Q winning. What are your two discards?

Problem 5.4
East/West Game. Dealer North.

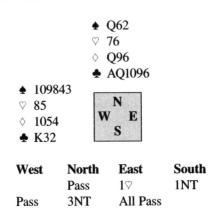

♠ Q62
♥ 76
⋄ Q96
♣ AQ1096

♠ 109843
♥ 85
⋄ 1054
♣ K32

West	North	East	South
	Pass	1♥	1NT
Pass	3NT	All Pass	

You lead the ♥8 to the ♥6, ♥10 and ♥2. Partner continues with the ♥A and ♥Q, South's ♥K winning. What do you discard?

Problem 5.5
East/West Game. Dealer North.

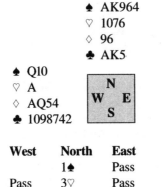

♠ AK964
♥ 1076
⋄ 96
♣ AK5

♠ Q10
♥ A
⋄ AQ54
♣ 1098742

West	North	East	South
	1♠	Pass	2♥
Pass	3♥	Pass	4♥
All Pass			

You lead the ♣10 to the ♣A, ♣Q, and ♣3. Dummy plays a heart to your ♥A, partner playing the ♥2, and wins the second round of clubs as East follows with the ♣J and South the ♣6. On the second round of trumps partner follows with the ♥4 and South wins with the ♥J. What do you discard?

Solutions

Problem 5.1

Partner's ♠2 clearly indicates clubs which seems a bit unlikely with all four top honours on view. If declarer has the ♣10, he is good for five tricks and there is little to be done, but if you trust him for that card, as you should, you will throw your ♣Q:

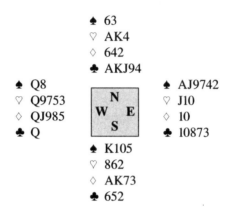

```
              ♠ 63
              ♥ AK4
              ◇ 642
              ♣ AKJ94
  ♠ Q8                        ♠ AJ9742
  ♥ Q9753      N              ♥ J10
  ◇ QJ985    W   E            ◇ 10
  ♣ Q          S              ♣ 10873
              ♠ K105
              ♥ 862
              ◇ AK73
              ♣ 652
```

If you keep the ♣Q, South will play a low club and allow your honour to hold, ensuring four club tricks to go with four top red cards and the spade. Once you have discarded the ♣Q, South is held to three club tricks and is a trick short. Or is he??? I asked whether you had any further comment and you should not take any credit unless you realised that, even after this excellent defence, the hand is far from over. What are going to discard on three top clubs? Looking at the deal, you can see that it is safe to throw two hearts and one diamond to keep parity with South with East being 6214 and South 3343. However, for all you know, East could just as easily have been 6124 and South 3433. Now discarding too many hearts allows South to set up an extra trick in that suit. You can't tell for sure, but South might have made a negative double with four hearts, so you should discard two hearts.

Problem 5.2

This one really hurts, but partner has played a middling heart on the third round of the suit and, like it or not, he is indicating the middle-ranking of the non-heart suits, i.e. diamonds. His entry must be the ◇J and you must unblock the position by throwing your ◇A away immediately:

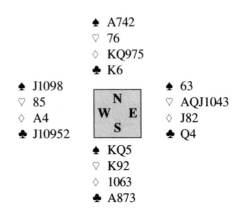

♠ A742
♡ 76
◇ KQ975
♣ K6

♠ J1098
♡ 85
◇ A4
♣ J10952

♠ 63
♡ AQJ1043
◇ J82
♣ Q4

♠ KQ5
♡ K92
◇ 1063
♣ A873

Now South is held to two clubs, the heart, two diamonds and three spades for eight tricks only. Keep your ◇A and he can lead the suit twice towards dummy, losing just one trick in it to your hand.

Problem 5.3

Sometimes you have the opportunity for two discards and it is just as well, as a double unblock is sometimes needed. This is a particularly difficult problem as you had to take the decision at trick two when you did not know what was coming at trick three. But a club can never cost and here you must get rid of both your honours in that suit to ensure that partner can win a club trick.

The deal:

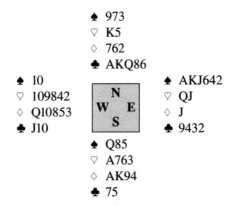

♠ 973
♡ K5
◇ 762
♣ AKQ86

♠ 10
♡ 109842
◇ Q10853
♣ J10

♠ AKJ642
♡ QJ
◇ J
♣ 9432

♠ Q85
♡ A763
◇ AK94
♣ 75

If you fail to do so, South can lead twice up to dummy's clubs and allow your ♣J to hold, ensuring four clubs, the spade and four red-suit tops. Get rid of both clubs and he is restricted to three clubs only and therefore eight tricks in total. You will, of course, closely follow declarer's discards on the clubs and also how partner follows to the ♣AKQ, high-low to indicate 6214 or low-high for 6142. Actually, you can be even more accurate:

> ♣4 ♣3 ♣2 for 6304 heavy emphasis on hearts
> ♣4 ♣2 ♣3 for 6214 moderate emphasis on hearts
> ♣2 ♣3 ♣4 for 6034 heavy emphasis on diamonds
> ♣2 ♣4 ♣3 for 6124 moderate emphasis on diamonds

Even in world-class bridge, I know of no pair who are that meticulous, but it shows how much information you can exchange in defence.

In practice, double unblocks of this kind are very rare, but it is worth being aware of their existence. Sometimes it is even worth sacrificing a trick to get partner in to cash several more winners. Above, we saw the discard of a jack and ten. But we could have anything up to:

♣ Q109875

♣ AK3   ♣ J4

♣ 62

Here West has to throw both his top cards to create an entry for East.

Problem 5.4

Well, did you discard the ♣K to get out of the way of partner's ♣J? You did? If so, shame on you! Partner, with his high ♡Q, was clearly asking for spades. The deal:

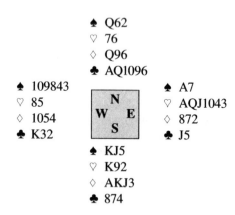

```
                    ♠ Q62
                    ♡ 76
                    ◊ Q96
                    ♣ AQ1096
    ♠ 109843          ┌─────────┐         ♠ A7
    ♡ 85              │    N    │         ♡ AQJ1043
    ◊ 1054            │  W   E  │         ◊ 872
    ♣ K32             │    S    │         ♣ J5
                      └─────────┘
                    ♠ KJ5
                    ♡ K92
                    ◊ AKJ3
                    ♣ 874
```

Now there is no need to be clever. Hold on to your clubs and wait patiently for a two-trick defeat.

Problem 5.5

You have already taken the ♡A and will need three more tricks. One possibility is to find partner with the ◊K, but in that case, South would be very short on points for his bidding. It is a near certainty that the ◊K is with South and that you will have to hope that he cannot set those spades up without partner getting in. To make the necessary arrangements, you will have to credit South with three low spades and partner with ♠Jxx. Even now, you are in trouble.

Suppose you throw a minor-suit card now. South will play a low spade and await developments. If you play the ♠Q, she will be allowed to hold and partner will be kept out of mischief. If you play low, dummy will win and now declarer will ruff dummy's last club and lead another low spade, allowing your ♠Q to hold. You will have to play a fourth round of clubs which South will win, draw any outstanding trumps and cash the spades:

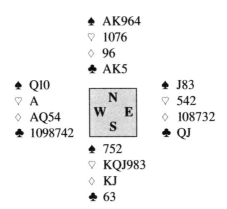

♠ AK964
♥ 1076
⋄ 96
♣ AK5

♠ Q10
♥ A
⋄ AQ54
♣ 1098742

♠ J83
♥ 542
⋄ 108732
♣ QJ

♠ 752
♥ KQJ983
⋄ KJ
♣ 63

To avert this, you must throw your ♠Q now, leaving partner in sole control of the suit. Nothing now can prevent the defence from scoring the ♠J and two diamonds. Declarer can get home with a different order of play. He should take three rounds of clubs at the start, ruffing the third. Now a low spade follows and you must play low to have any chance. Dummy wins and plays a trump, losing to your ♥A. If you play the ♠Q now, she is allowed to hold and it is all over. A diamond also amounts to throwing in the towel so it has to be a fourth round of clubs, giving a ruff and discard.

So, in these examples we have learnt how and when to discard to unblock suits for partner's benefit. Although it is outside the scope of this book, the vast majority of unblocking plays occur when one is following suit rather than discarding. An example has already appeared earlier in the book. Remember this hand from Chapter 2?

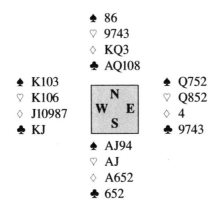

♠ 86
♥ 9743
⋄ KQ3
♣ AQ108

♠ K103
♥ K106
⋄ J10987
♣ KJ

♠ Q752
♥ Q852
⋄ 4
♣ 9743

♠ AJ94
♥ AJ
⋄ A652
♣ 652

South was in 3NT and you were East, facing partner's lead of the ◊J. Dummy won and a spade went to the ♠9 and ♠10. I asked for your discard on the second round of diamonds and explained that a heart was preferable to a club. However, if you do discard a heart, declarer can turn his attention to that suit. Now if he plays the ♡A and ♡J, East must toss in his ♡Q under the ♡A or under the ♡K so that his partner wins both defensive tricks in that suit and is consequently able to set up and cash his diamonds. If East wins a heart trick, the contract cannot be beaten. This is a very difficult defence to find at the table, but of course, it is unlikely that declarer would play like this anyway before testing clubs. But this is all worth bearing in mind.

In all the examples I have given you, I placed you in the West seat, unblocking in front of a visible dummy. It is, of course, far more difficult to do so as East in front of a closed hand. This is a good example, which few defenders, if any, would get right:

Game All. Dealer South.

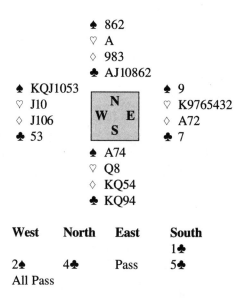

	♠ 862	
	♡ A	
	◊ 983	
	♣ AJ10862	
♠ KQJ1053		♠ 9
♡ J10		♡ K9765432
◊ J106		◊ A72
♣ 53		♣ 7
	♠ A74	
	♡ Q8	
	◊ KQ54	
	♣ KQ94	

West	North	East	South
			1♣
2♠	4♣	Pass	5♣
All Pass			

The weak jump overcall by West, at this vulnerability, promises a very good suit.

West led the ♠K, won by South. South now played two rounds of trumps, ending in dummy, and then led a low diamond. How should you defend as East?

Too late if you are still thinking. You had to get rid of that ◊A on the second club to leave declarer a trick short. If you did not, he can play on diamonds, losing to your (safe) hand, eventually discarding a losing spade on the fourth round. But discard your ◊A and the lost trick in the suit will now go to West who can cash his two spade winners in time. If declarer had foreseen the danger, he would cross to dummy in clubs at trick two for a diamond, which East must duck and then cross to dummy in hearts for a second diamond. (Alternatively he could cross to dummy in hearts twice.) Now East is helpless. Of course, at the table, South did not dream that the club shortage was with East!

I think that will be enough on unblocking declarer's long suits. We now have to consider positions where declarer is threatening an endplay and we shall learn again that there are many situations where high cards are best disposed of at an early stage.

Chapter 6

Avoiding Embarrassment in the Endgame

In this chapter, particular emphasis will be laid on anticipating the play from an early stage. Not only will you have to visualise situations in which you are going to be endplayed, but also those in which partner might suffer a similar fate. Obviously, which defender wins tricks will often make all the difference. So important is this point, that I spent a whole chapter on it in my beginners' book so that those learning the game from scratch would realise that it is not necessarily right to play the lowest card when following to a trick which you have no chance of winning.

This was typical of a two-card position I discussed:

$$\clubsuit\ 94$$
$$\clubsuit\ KJ \qquad \qquad \clubsuit\ Q2$$
$$\clubsuit\ A6$$

In this layout, it is clear that declarer will win one trick and the defenders one. Declarer's trick will obviously be won by South. But if he starts with the ♣A, the defenders have a choice. Throwing the ♣J will result in West winning the second round, but if West is determined to get his partner in, he will contribute the king under the ace. Note that, if declarer starts the suit from dummy he can keep East out of the lead. If East plays low, so does South, forcing West to win. If East rises with the ♣Q, South wins and now West is forced to win the second round. So South may be able to keep East off play, but cannot keep West off play in any circumstances.

Bridge hands are full with situations like this and, in the world of the endplay, defenders must plan their discards so that they keep the correct holdings to avoid one of them having to make an embarrassing lead.

Guiding principle

If a declarer has a tenace position, make every effort to arrange to win the trick in the endplay position if you are sitting under the tenace. Conversely, make every effort to arrange for partner to win the trick if you are sitting over the tenace.

So taking the diamond suit as example, suppose we have this everyday situation:

◇ AKJ

◇ 8653   ◇ Q102

◇ 974

If East can be forced to open up the suit, South will escape a loser. If West can lead it, South is forced into the finesse, losing on the lie of the cards.

We shall look at some examples, first seeing all four hands. As always, making the seven roll-calls will be crucial:

Game All. Dealer East.

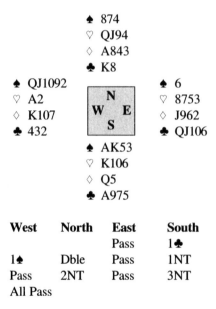

♠ 874
♡ QJ94
◇ A843
♣ K8

♠ QJ1092   ♠ 6
♡ A2   ♡ 8753
◇ K107   ◇ J962
♣ 432   ♣ QJ106

♠ AK53
♡ K106
◇ Q5
♣ A975

West	North	East	South
		Pass	1♣
1♠	Dble	Pass	1NT
Pass	2NT	Pass	3NT
All Pass			

North's double was negative, seeking a four-four fit in hearts. South showed 15-16 high-card points and then confirmed a maximum in that range.

West led the ♠Q, won by South who now played the ♡K. There was nothing to be gained by ducking, indeed it could be vital to win if East held ♡10xxx. So West won and persisted with spades. East discarded a low heart as South won. Now followed three more hearts, on which South discarded a club and West had to find two discards. He could easily afford two of those dazzling clubs and did not give the matter a second thought, blissfully unaware that he had presented South with his contract. South cashed two rounds of clubs and exited in spades. West was thus allowed to cash his three winners, but then had to lead away from his ◊K, giving South his ninth trick. Who would have thought that West cannot afford even one club discard, never mind two?

We shall roll-call the hand and see what we can find out. West and dummy have ten points each, leaving twenty unaccounted for, of which we know East has four. South has already shown the two top spades and the ♡K, ten so far. If he has both ◊QJ, the ◊K is dead and there is no hope so credit at least one of them to East so that one diamond discard is clearly affordable. Declarer has two spade tricks and three hearts, five so far, and cannot be denied the ◊A for a sixth. Giving East the ◊J at least, South must have the ♣A, giving him at least two tricks in that suit for eight and partner will need the ♣Q and ♣J for the defence to have a chance.

Now it seems difficult to realise this, but that third little club, facing ♣QJ and others, is actually a *winner* and must be held so that East can be put on play to lead a diamond through. The tenace is split on this occasion, but the ◊Q is the important card and West, sitting over it, must hold his clubs and arrange for his partner to win that crucial third round of clubs. West must discard a diamond and a winning spade. The same would have applied if South had held the ◊A, effectively:

```
                    ◊ 84
         ◊ K10                ◊ J9
                    ◊ AQ
```

instead of:

```
                    ◊ A8
         ◊ K10                ◊ J9
                    ◊ Q5
```

This is not an easy hand, but I include it because, although the vast majority of players do not realise it, deals of this type occur daily. Contracts are regularly presented to undeserving declarers through defenders religiously holding on to their winners and totally neglecting possible winners in their partner's hand as above.

We shall look at another 3NT contract where again you are sitting West, but must be careful that partner is not put on lead at the wrong moment:

Love All. Dealer West.

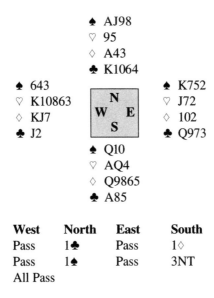

```
                    ♠ AJ98
                    ♡ 95
                    ◇ A43
                    ♣ K1064
     ♠ 643                        ♠ K752
     ♡ K10863        N            ♡ J72
     ◇ KJ7       W     E          ◇ 102
     ♣ J2           S             ♣ Q973
                    ♠ Q10
                    ♡ AQ4
                    ◇ Q9865
                    ♣ A85
```

West	North	East	South
Pass	1♣	Pass	1◇
Pass	1♠	Pass	3NT
All Pass			

Note that I strongly recommend 1♣ rather than 1NT on the North cards. You have an easy rebid of 1♠ and, with 3NT hot favourite as final contract if game be reached, you will, looking at both red-suit holdings, want the declaration from the other side. The hearts here are a case in point. But partner could also have had something like ◇Qx.

West led the ♡6 and East's ♡J lost to South's ♡Q. South played a diamond to the ◇A and a second round to the ◇Q and ◇K. West's ♡K held and, winning the third round of hearts, dummy discarding a diamond, South tried the spade finesse, but East won and returned the suit. Declarer cashed the remaining spades, discarding low diamonds from his own hand. On the last, this was the position with West still to discard:

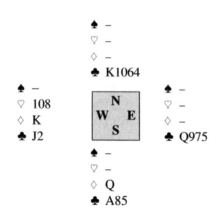

Declarer has won three spade tricks, two hearts and one diamond, six in all so far, for the loss of one diamond, one heart and one spade, three. Obviously he has two clubs to come. Clearly the ◊K cannot be spared, but it is not so apparent that throwing a club is also fatal. The ♣4 is led to the ♣A and the next round is ducked to East, who is now endplayed. The safe discard is a winning heart. Now South is forced to win the second club and it is now dummy who is endplayed. What West had to ask himself is: 'How many rounds of clubs will be played?' Answer: 'at least two.' Therefore hold two clubs – it cannot cost and might gain.

Very often, in this type of situation against a no-trump contract, a defender will have to discard an established winner in the endgame. It seems heartbreaking after all that hard work, but it pays to be aware that apparent losers (as the ♣J above) in declarer's suit can be far more important.

We have seen two examples; one where you had to protect yourself from being endplayed and a second where you had to protect your partner. In the examples that follow you will first have to decide who is the potential sufferer and then see to it that you hold on to the appropriate cards to avoid trouble.

Quiz on avoiding endplays

Problem 6.1
Love All. Dealer East.

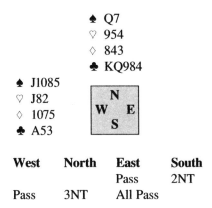

♠ Q7
♡ 954
◇ 843
♣ KQ984

♠ J1085
♡ J82
◇ 1075
♣ A53

West	North	East	South
		Pass	2NT
Pass	3NT	All Pass	

You lead the ♠J to the ♠Q, ♠K and ♠A. South cashes three top diamonds, partner following with ◇2, ◇6, ◇9, and then cashes the ◇J. No doubt, partner is able to give an informative discard on this, but it is your turn first! What do you throw and why?

Problem 6.2
North/South Game. Dealer East.

♠ AK92
♡ K54
◇ Q432
♣ 84

♠ QJ7
♡ 108762
◇ K9
♣ 752

West	North	East	South
		Pass	1♡
Pass	1♠	2NT	Pass
3♣	3♡	Pass	4♡
All Pass			

Partner showed at least 5-5 in the minors. You lead the ◊K, which holds, as partner encourages with the ◊8. On the second round, partner's ◊10 wins and he switches to the ♣Q, won by South with the ♣A. Now comes the ♠6 to dummy's ♠K. The ♡K is cashed, partner discarding a diamond, followed by the ♣K and a club ruff. Now a diamond is covered with the ◊J and ruffed by South with the ♡J. What is your discard?

Problem 6.3
North/South Game. Dealer West.

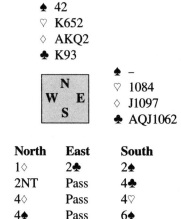

```
              ♠ 42
              ♡ K652
              ◊ AKQ2
              ♣ K93
                         ♠ –
              N          ♡ 1084
          W       E      ◊ J1097
              S          ♣ AQJ1062
```

West	North	East	South
Pass	1◊	2♣	2♠
Pass	2NT	Pass	4♣
Pass	4◊	Pass	4♡
Pass	4♠	Pass	6♠
All Pass			

South's jump in opponents' suit showed a void and a self-supporting spade suit. Cue-bidding followed.

Partner leads the ♣8 to the ♣9 and ♣10. South ruffs and lays down the ♠A. Partner follows, but what do you discard?

Problem 6.4
North/South Game. Dealer South.

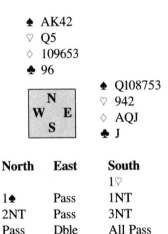

```
              ♠ AK42
              ♡ Q5
              ◇ 109653
              ♣ 96
                              ♠ Q108753
                              ♡ 942
                              ◇ AQJ
                              ♣ J
```

West	North	East	South
			1♡
Pass	1♠	Pass	1NT
Pass	2NT	Pass	3NT
Pass	Pass	Dble	All Pass

South's rebid promised 15-16 points so he will be maximum in that range.

With opponents having crawled up to their game, you decide to throw in the red card for a spade lead and partner produces the ♠9. This runs to your ♠Q and South's ♠J. Dummy wins the second round, South discarding a low diamond, and a diamond is played to your ◇Q and South's ◇K. You win the second round of diamonds with the ◇A, as West discards the ♣4, and persist with spades, dummy winning as South discards another diamond and West the ♣3. Now follow four rounds of hearts, South having started with ♡AKJ10. West follows up the line, dummy discarding diamonds, and on the fourth round you can see:

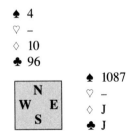

```
              ♠ 4
              ♡ -
              ◇ 10
              ♣ 96
                              ♠ 1087
                              ♡ -
                              ◇ J
                              ♣ J
```

What do you discard now?

Problem 6.5
North/South Game. Dealer South.

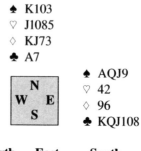

          ♠ K103
          ♡ J1085
          ◊ KJ73
          ♣ A7
                              ♠ AQJ9
                              ♡ 42
                              ◊ 96
                              ♣ KQJ108

West	North	East	South
			1♡
Pass	2◊	Dble	2NT
Pass	4♡	All Pass	

After your double, South's 2NT showed a good constructive raise to 3◊. Bidding 3◊ direct would have been preemptive and with a genuine 2NT rebid, South would have redoubled.

West leads the ♠6 and dummy's ♠10 is played. Your ♠J wins, as South plays the ♠2. You switch to the ♣K, won in dummy, partner playing the ♣5 and declarer the ♣2. Three rounds of trumps follow, partner playing ♡6, ♡7 and ♡9. Now declarer cashes four rounds of diamonds, partner following with ◊4, ◊5 and ◊8, then discarding the ♠8. You have to find three discards on the seven rounds of red suits. What are they?

Solutions

Problem 6.1

As always, the seven roll-calls will save you from disaster. Declarer has already shown the ♠A and four diamond winners, five tricks so far from fourteen points. Partner's carding in diamonds has indicated that he cannot help in spades. The crucial questions are: 'What is his heart holding?' and 'How many clubs has he?' If partner has the ♡A, declarer is booked for defeat unless he has ♠A9xx. He will have to cross to dummy twice to lead up to his hearts, so he will need three clubs. If he has three clubs, your defence will be irrelevant. Where South has the ♡A, then even giving him the ♣J, he will need at least one of the other heart honours to reach a minimum of twenty points. That gives him two heart tricks to add to the five already won, implying that again, if he has three clubs, you have no defence.

So South will have to be credited with a doubleton club. That gives you the vital clue. You can now spare a club and keep your major-suit holdings intact. Observe the effect of discarding a heart: South will (crossing to dummy once if necessary to take a finesse) cash two hearts and then concentrate on clubs, forcing you to win and lead spades round to him. Keep all your hearts, however, and you will have the third heart as exit card and be able to get partner in to lead a spade:

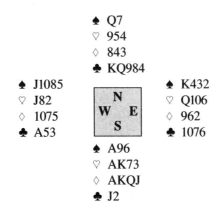

```
            ♠ Q7
            ♡ 954
            ◇ 843
            ♣ KQ984
 ♠ J1085              ♠ K432
 ♡ J82      N         ♡ Q106
 ◇ 1075   W   E       ◇ 962
 ♣ A53      S         ♣ 1076
            ♠ A96
            ♡ AK73
            ◇ AKQJ
            ♣ J2
```

Problem 6.2

It seems obvious to discard a 'losing' spade, but your second spade is a winner rather than a loser. If you do, declarer will simply play the ♠A and another spade, forcing you to ruff. Now you will have to play another trump round to South's tenace, giving him the contract. So try the effect of underruffing. Now, when declarer plays a spade, you put in the ♠Q, so that partner can win the third round while you are still following. Now any minor-suit card from him will ensure a trick for your ♡10. Of course, there is no defence if you failed to contribute a spade *honour* when the suit was first played, retaining the seven as a potential exit card:

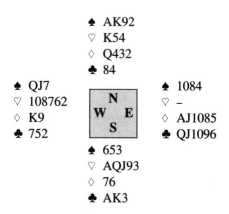

```
                    ♠ AK92
                    ♡ K54
                    ◇ Q432
                    ♣ 84
     ♠ QJ7                        ♠ 1084
     ♡ 108762        N            ♡ –
     ◇ K9         W     E         ◇ AJ1085
     ♣ 752           S            ♣ QJ1096
                    ♠ 653
                    ♡ AQJ93
                    ◇ 76
                    ♣ AK3
```

Problem 6.3

Can you see the danger? This is the corollary of the last problem seen from partner's point of view. If South's spades are solid, there is probably little to discuss, but if they are not, the position might be as below:

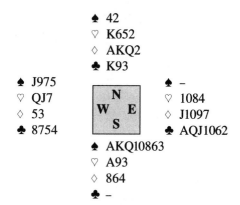

```
                    ♠ 42
                    ♡ K652
                    ◇ AKQ2
                    ♣ K93
     ♠ J975                       ♠ –
     ♡ QJ7           N            ♡ 1084
     ◇ 53         W     E         ◇ J1097
     ♣ 8754          S            ♣ AQJ1062
                    ♠ AKQ10863
                    ♡ A93
                    ◇ 864
                    ♣ –
```

You see what is going to happen. Declarer will cross twice in diamonds to ruff two more clubs, reducing his spade length to that of West's. He can even play a third round of diamonds from hand. Now, if West ruffs, declarer claims because the heart loser goes on the fourth diamond – just the one trump trick is lost. So West discards a club and eventually declarer will play three rounds of hearts, hoping to lose the last round to West. Stuck with nothing but trumps, he has to give up what looked like an unassailable trick. You have to see to it that the third heart is won in your hand, i.e. that partner has the ♡Q and ♡J and will throw them on the first two rounds of the suit. I asked what you would discard on the first trump. I should, of course, have asked what do you *not* discard. You must hang on to all those red cards at all costs. A club is safe.

Problem 6.4

Declarer has taken four heart tricks, two spades and a diamond for seven tricks and has shown ♡AKJ, the ◊K and ♠J, totalling twelve points. Four are thus unaccounted for and they must be the ♣A:

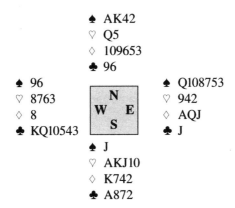

```
              ♠ AK42
              ♡ Q5
              ◊ 109653
              ♣ 96
♠ 96                        ♠ Q108753
♡ 8763      N               ♡ 942
◊ 8       W   E             ◊ AQJ
♣ KQ10543   S               ♣ J
              ♠ J
              ♡ AKJ10
              ◊ K742
              ♣ A872
```

You can now see the danger. You must, at all costs, hang on to that ♣J. You see what will happen if you discard it. The early play will have enabled South to read your distribution and he will now play a low club, unblocking the ♣9 as West is forced to win. He will duck the next club honour, leaving partner endplayed in the suit. To avoid this, you must keep the ♣J so that you can win the first round and cash your winners.

As the cards lie, you can actually discard either the ◊J or a spade. But the spade is safer.

Note that West did not discard a heart early on. South was known to have at least four hearts and you could have held ♡J109. Partner was following the rule of maintaining parity with South.

Problem 6.5

It would have been more appropriate if I had asked what you should *not* discard. The one card you must hang on to is the ♣8! Can you see what is threatening? After the diamonds, declarer will exit in clubs and, if you win, you will have to present declarer with a spade trick or play another club, giving him a ruff and discard for his tenth trick:

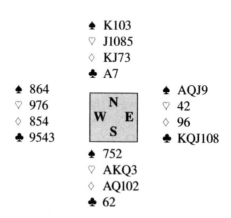

       ♠ K103
       ♡ J1085
       ◇ KJ73
       ♣ A7

♠ 864   ♠ AQJ9
♡ 976   **N**   ♡ 42
◇ 854   **W   E**   ◇ 96
♣ 9543   **S**   ♣ KQJ108

       ♠ 752
       ♡ AKQ3
       ◇ AQ102
       ♣ 62

Keep the ♣8, however, and you can allow partner's only decent card, the ♣9 to win the second round of clubs and now a second spade through dummy will seal declarer's doom.

From this problem, we can lay down a further tip:

> **Guiding principle**
>
> If you need to assume that partner has a certain card to avoid you being endplayed, play on the assumption that he has it.

For our next chapter, we are going to use the knowledge we have acquired in previous chapters to study the most difficult area of the game; squeeze defence.

Chapter 7

In the Pressure Cooker

All too often defenders find themselves forced to discard from embarrassing holdings. Typically, after eight tricks have been played in a spade contract, you find yourself holding something like:

♠ –
♡ K8
◇ Q63
♣ –

Now that confounded declarer leads a black card. Like it or not, the irrepressible force has met the unstoppable block and something has to go. However, we have learnt that these positions are not necessarily hopeless in that you have a partner who may be able to help. There may be a blockage preventing declarer from enjoying his full compliment of winners despite your 'help' or some other reason which will make it safe for you to blank one of your honours.

What you need to do now is to learn to recognise which suit is vital to hold and which can be weakened and leads us to our first tip:

Guiding Principle

If you are under pressure in two or three suits, and have to abandon one of them, it will usually be right to abandon it completely rather than fall between two stools.

Be warned that this is not clear-cut in that it may, for example, be worthwhile keeping a singleton honour to protect partner against a finesse. However, your first priority should be to keep one suit properly guarded.

This is a typical hand in which defenders failed to cooperate:

Game All. Dealer East.

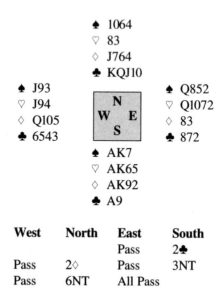

West	North	East	South
		Pass	2♣
Pass	2♢	Pass	3NT
Pass	6NT	All Pass	

West selected a safe ♣6 for his opening lead, won in declarer's hand. South tried two top diamonds and then a third round, won by West, as East, trying to delay the inevitable, discarded a club. West played another club and now declarer cashed his remaining clubs. East could afford one card from each major without sweat, and South pitched a spade and a diamond:

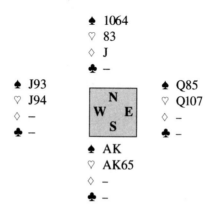

On the last club, East was faced with a terrible decision. Assuming that, at this point, declarer had probably come down to three cards in each major, East discarded another heart. South discarded a heart and now the spotlight fell on West. From his point of view, his partner, who had thrown the ♡2 followed by the ♠2, had probably started with five hearts and three spades. Therefore, declarer was down to three spades and two hearts, so West also let go of a heart, presenting South with his twelfth trick.

Declarer played the hand cleverly, but East/West provided very poor defence. East just focused on his own problem without realising that his partner could help but needed accurate information in order to do so. However, this kind of thing happens daily. Although the example above resulted in an enormous loss, the commonest penalty is in the pairs' event at your local club where crucial overtricks are chucked by the millions in this kind of situation.

Before proceeding further, it will be helpful to lay down another relevant tip, which would have helped the defence on the previous hand:

Guiding Principle

Squeezes usually threaten in high-level contracts where the defenders have poor cards. In that case, it is usually right for defenders to give each other information on count wherever possible. It will usually be obvious what few high cards they have between them.

So we shall replay the above hand on that basis. East's first two major-suit discards should have been the ♡7 and ♠8. Now West will be in control of the situation, since he will have an accurate count of the hand. Whichever suit East then abandons, West can hold on to. Alternatively, he can simply come down to the same shape as declarer.

In our second example, the necessity of giving count is illustrated again:

East/West Game. Dealer North.

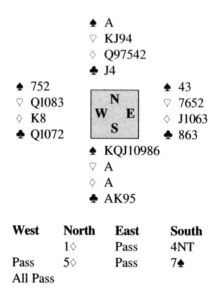

```
              ♠ A
              ♡ KJ94
              ◇ Q97542
              ♣ J4
♠ 752                        ♠ 43
♡ Q1083        N             ♡ 7652
◇ K8        W     E          ◇ J1063
♣ Q1072        S             ♣ 863
              ♠ KQJ10986
              ♡ A
              ◇ A
              ♣ AK95
```

West	North	East	South
	1◇	Pass	4NT
Pass	5◇	Pass	7♠
All Pass			

Feeling embarrassed to touch a side-suit, West hit the jackpot with a trump lead, cutting declarer's communications. Dummy won, perforce, and declarer crossed to his ♡A, East playing the ♡2, to run the rest of the trumps. It is very easy to defend seeing the full deal, but, already on the fifth round, West was in trouble; this is what he could see:

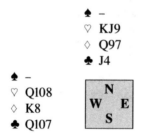

```
              ♠ –
              ♡ KJ9
              ◇ Q97
              ♣ J4
♠ –
♡ Q108         N
◇ K8        W     E
♣ Q107         S
```

He knew that two more trumps were still to come, but he had not paid sufficient attention to his partner's discards and decided to play East for the ♣9, throwing a second club and allowing the grand slam to make.

Despite the 'mistake' of the ♡2, giving a misleading count on that suit, East was able to save his partner a headache very easily. He could have discarded his three clubs up the line to give West an accurate count in that suit. Now West can safely count South for 7114, keep his clubs and abandon both red suits. Alternatively, East could have rectified his earlier error by discarding three more hearts, again giving count in that suit so that West could place South with a stiff ♡A. He can now throw his hearts easily.

However, in any event, West should have realised that, if South had a second heart, the finesse against the ♡Q was working, leaving South with seven trump tricks, three hearts and surely three top tricks in the minors (if his bidding made any sense) to complete thirteen tricks.

Notice again how the application of the seven roll-calls prevents countless mistakes.

These examples should have given you the idea of how defenders can cooperate to avoid throwing the wrong cards in squeeze positions. Countless books have been written on squeezes and obviously discussions on squeeze defence have been exhaustively included. Many test examples have been offered, including some very difficult ones. However, to start with, I should like you try the following five fairly straightforward problems.

Quiz on basic squeeze defence

Problem 7.1
North/South Game. Dealer South.

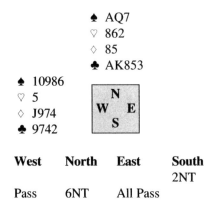

```
              ♠ AQ7
              ♡ 862
              ◇ 85
              ♣ AK853
  ♠ 10986      ┌─────────┐
  ♡ 5          │    N    │
  ◇ J974       │  W   E  │
  ♣ 9742       │    S    │
              └─────────┘
```

West	North	East	South
			2NT
Pass	6NT	All Pass	

You lead the ♠10 to the ♠Q, ♠K and ♠2. Partner returns the ♠4, South winning with the ♠J. Declarer continues with the ♡A, partner following with ♡7. On the ♡K, you can easily afford a spade, as partner plays the ♡9. On the ♡Q, you can discard your last spade, partner playing the ♡4. But what are you going to throw on the ♡J, bearing in mind that declarer can put you to still further embarrassment with a third round of spades?

Problem 7.2
North/South Game. Dealer West.

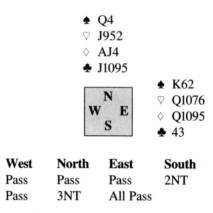

♠ Q4
♡ J952
◇ AJ4
♣ J1095

♠ K62
♡ Q1076
◇ Q1095
♣ 43

West	North	East	South
Pass	Pass	Pass	2NT
Pass	3NT	All Pass	

Partner leads the ♠J to the ♠Q, ♠K and ♠3. On your ♠6, South covers with the ♠7 and West's ♠10 wins. His ♠9 forces declarer's ♠A, as dummy discards a low diamond. Now follow a low club to the ♣J and two more high clubs, partner following with the ♣2, ♣8 and ♣7. What do you discard on third round, bearing in mind that you may have to find a further discard on a fourth round of clubs?

Problem 7.3
East/West Game. Dealer East.

♠ A62
♡ AJ963
◇ Q952
♣ 4

♠ K985
♡ 5
◇ 873
♣ KJ1072

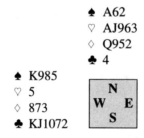

West	North	East	South
		Pass	1♡
Pass	4♣	Pass	4NT
Pass	5♡	Pass	6♡
All Pass			

You lead the ◊7 and dummy's ◊2 is played. Partner wins with the ◊A, South playing the ◊10, and returns the ◊6, won by South's ◊K. South cashes the ♣A and ruffs a club in dummy, partner following with the ♣3 and ♣6, before drawing two rounds of trumps, partner following with the ♡4 and ♡7. Now South overtakes his ◊J in dummy and cashes a fourth round, discarding a low spade from hand. Then follow two more rounds of trumps, East discarding the ♣8 and ♣9 to complete ten tricks leaving:

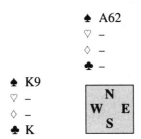

```
              ♠ A62
              ♡ –
              ◊ –
              ♣ –
   ♠ K9
   ♡ –       ┌─────────┐
   ◊ –       │    N    │
   ♣ K       │  W   E  │
             │    S    │
             └─────────┘
```

Now South plays his last trump. What do you discard?

Problem 7.4
North/South Game. Dealer South.

```
              ♠ AQ9
              ♡ QJ73
              ◊ A652
              ♣ K3
             ┌─────────┐   ♠ K43
             │    N    │   ♡ 64
             │  W   E  │   ◊ J1097
             │    S    │   ♣ 8752
             └─────────┘
```

West	North	East	South
			2NT
Pass	7NT	All Pass	

Partner leads the ♣10 and dummy's ♣K wins. South now cashes the ♡A and ♡K and then a third round to dummy's ♡Q while partner plays the ♡9, ♡5 and ♡8. The ♡J is now cashed. What are your two discards?

Problem 7.5
North/South Game. Dealer West.

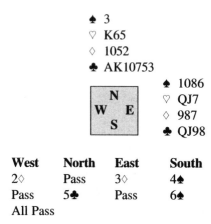

```
        ♠ 3
        ♡ K65
        ◇ 1052
        ♣ AK10753
                        ♠ 1086
                        ♡ QJ7
                        ◇ 987
                        ♣ QJ98
```

West	North	East	South
2◇	Pass	3◇	4♠
Pass	5♣	Pass	6♠
All Pass			

Your partnership is playing weak twos in all three non-club suits.

West leads two top diamonds, South ruffing the second round. West follows to two rounds of trumps, discarding the ◇4 on the third. On the fourth round, he discards the ◇6 and you can easily spare your last diamond. On the fifth round West discards the ◇3 and, with dummy having thrown one heart, two clubs and its last diamond, you can now see:

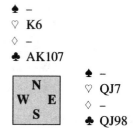

```
        ♠ –
        ♡ K6
        ◇ –
        ♣ AK107
                        ♠ –
                        ♡ QJ7
                        ◇ –
                        ♣ QJ98
```

Your hand is still to play. What do you discard now?

Solutions

Problem 7.1

The crucial point here is to back the horse which has a chance, against the one which must lose. On the bidding, South is marked with at least a doubleton club and that leaves East with at most two cards in that suit. Abandoning clubs, therefore, is a certain loser, irrespective of how the outstanding cards lie. However, you may find partner with some help in diamonds and you should discard twice from that suit:

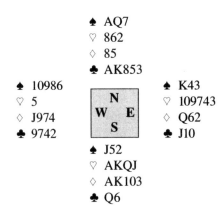

```
                    ♠ AQ7
                    ♡ 862
                    ◇ 85
                    ♣ AK853
   ♠ 10986                        ♠ K43
   ♡ 5           ┌─────────┐      ♡ 109743
   ◇ J974        │   N     │      ◇ Q62
   ♣ 9742        │ W   E   │      ♣ J10
                 │   S     │
                 └─────────┘
                    ♠ J52
                    ♡ AKQJ
                    ◇ AK103
                    ♣ Q6
```

Your ◇J will protect partner from a finesse, but it only needs to be guarded once. Notice partner's carding in hearts was designed to help you. He knew that he could not help in clubs and therefore played high hearts ♡7, ♡9, ♡4, confirming the odd number (low-high on the first two rounds) and then that his interest was in the higher-ranking of the two minor suits.

As the opportunity for this sort of signal is commonly missed even by top-class players, it can be summed up in the following tip:

Guiding Principle

When it is clear that you are going to be able to follow with low cards several times on declarer's long running suit, and it is clear that partner is going to come under pressure, then, unless you are sure that giving information will be more helpful to declarer, take the opportunity to give as much information as possible, especially regarding which suits you can stop and which you cannot.

Problem 7.2

This looks like a very unpleasant decision. South appears to have four club tricks, the ♠A already made, the ◊A and probably the ♡A for seven tricks to date. If you discard a diamond and South has four cards in that suit, he can take a losing finesse into your hand and thereby set up a long card in his own hand, using the fourth club as entry. Against that, if you prefer a heart, it could turn out that South has ♡AKx and he could play three rounds, losing the third to you, but now dummy's long heart would be established, the ◊A being available as entry.

Fortunately, partner has already told you (twice!) what to do. The way he played the early spades was strange: ♠10 followed by ♠9. Also, after giving you count on clubs, he played his second and third rounds upside down, again suggesting (McKenney-style) the higher-ranking of the two outstanding i.e. red suits. You should trust him for a high heart and abandon that suit:

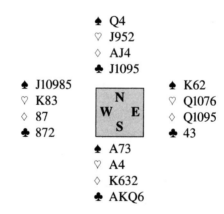

```
              ♠ Q4
              ♡ J952
              ◊ AJ4
              ♣ J1095
 ♠ J10985                    ♠ K62
 ♡ K83         N             ♡ Q1076
 ◊ 87        W   E           ◊ Q1095
 ♣ 872         S             ♣ 43
              ♠ A73
              ♡ A4
              ◊ K632
              ♣ AKQ6
```

Problem 7.3

The clue here is the count in clubs. Partner showed an odd number and, far more important, if South is still holding another club, he could have ruffed it in dummy hours ago before drawing trumps. Clearly, therefore, South started with 3532 and is still holding two spades. If they are the ♠Q and ♠J, there is no hope. If partner has the ♠Q, the contract is doomed. But declarer must have it to complete fifteen points. The critical case arises when partner has the ♠J when you can save the day by discarding your ♣K:

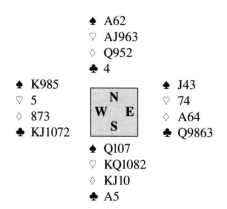

<pre>
                    ♠ A62
                    ♡ AJ963
                    ◇ Q952
                    ♣ 4
    ♠ K985   ♠ J43
    ♡ 5   ┌─────────┐   ♡ 74
    ◇ 873   │   N   │   ◇ A64
    ♣ KJ1072   │ W   E   │   ♣ Q9863
                │   S   │
                └─────────┘
                    ♠ Q107
                    ♡ KQ1082
                    ◇ KJ10
                    ♣ A5
</pre>

This is a very simple example and yet the number of people who would go wrong in this situation is staggering. We shall lay down a very obvious tip.

Guiding Principle

If declarer has an obvious opportunity to take ruffs in dummy in a given suit and fails to do so, you can assume that either he has no cards in hand to ruff or that the cards he does hold are winners and there is no need to ruff them. Use this information to count the hand.

Problem 7.4

It is clear from the bidding that, even giving him a minimum opener, South has all the remaining honours and thus he has four club tricks, four hearts, three diamonds and the ♠A to total twelve so far. He may go for the spade finesse for his thirteenth, failing as the cards lie, but he does not have to commit himself to that until much later. Can you see the trouble ahead? Suppose you discard two low clubs at this point. South will then test the diamonds, find, to his horror, that they are not breaking, and then cash the rest of the clubs. At trick ten, you will be down to ♠K4 and ◇J10 and something will have to go on the last club. What invariably happens in this situation is that the defender goes into a huddle and eventually and with obvious reluctance, discards the ♠4, making it obvious to declarer that his squeeze has been a success and the drop in spades should now be preferred to the finesse.

My suggestion is that you do not wait for the clubs, but discard two low spades now, showing obvious disinterest in the suit. Now when declarer cashes his winners, you will happily follow and it is now very likely that he will prefer the spade finesse, with nothing untoward having happened. You produce the ♠K – one off. After all, who on Earth blanks a king against a grand slam half way through the play when he does not have to?

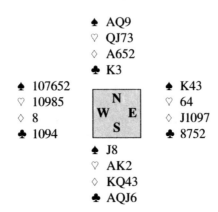

♠ AQ9
♡ QJ73
◇ A652
♣ K3

♠ 107652   ♠ K43
♡ 10985   ♡ 64
◇ 8   ◇ J1097
♣ 1094   ♣ 8752

♠ J8
♡ AK2
◇ KQ43
♣ AQJ6

This brings us to a good tip, which arises far more often than many players realise.

Guiding Principle

Indecent exposure – mornings only! If you can see that your hand is going to be squeezed and that, as a result, you will have to blank an honour, do it early in the play, i.e. before the pressure really bites, with obvious calm. Declarer is far less likely to suspect what you have really done. He will probably place the honour with your partner and may well misplay the hand as a result.

We saw an earlier example in Chapter 3 when you blanked the ◇Q down to a doubleton in a two-way finesse or drop position. During my career, I have got into the habit, notably against high-level contracts, of going out of my way to seek out these situations. The dividends have been incalculable. This hand leads us into the world of deception which, sadly, has to be left to another book.

Problem 7.5

This again is a problem of deciding which horse has a chance. Clearly South has the ♡A and, if he has the ♡10 as well, you are genuinely squeezed and helpless. Discarding a club is a definite loser. South will play three rounds, ruffing the third, and the fourth card in dummy will be established. Discarding a heart, however, may be better if partner can help with the ♡10 as here:

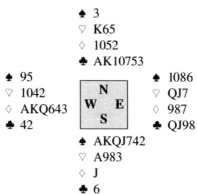

```
                  ♠ 3
                  ♡ K65
                  ◊ 1052
                  ♣ AK10753
   ♠ 95                          ♠ 1086
   ♡ 1042          N             ♡ QJ7
   ◊ AKQ643      W   E           ◊ 987
   ♣ 42            S             ♣ QJ98
                  ♠ AKQJ742
                  ♡ A983
                  ◊ J
                  ♣ 6
```

Notice partner vitally held on to all three of his hearts. As long as the ◊10 remains in dummy, he must hold his ◊Q, but the lower diamonds and the two low clubs can go. Yet a disturbing number of people would misdefend this hand from either side of the table. Note that, if there is no outside entry to dummy, it is only necessary for East to keep three clubs.

So far, we have considered straightforward simple-squeeze situations where you had a choice of two suits to discard. We are now going to proceed to more complex situations where declarer is playing for a double or triple squeeze. Again, counting and placing the unseen cards will obviously be crucial.

There are many variants of double-squeeze positions, but the usual scenario is that West is solely in charge of one suit and East is solely in charge of another with the result that neither is able to hold on to third. Here, in a no-trump contract (or diamonds could be trumps; it makes no difference) is a typical end-game matrix with declarer needing all the remaining tricks:

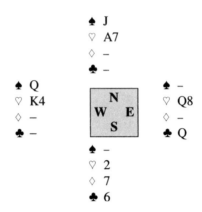

South has set up a long diamond suit and, on the last round, the defenders have no answer. West must throw a heart to keep his spade control intact. The ♣J, having completed its duty as 'menace' is now discarded from dummy, and East is in trouble. He must keep his club control so he too has to discard a heart. Declarer now makes both dummy's hearts.

The terminology here is that the black suits are described as 'single menaces,' i.e. held by one defender only, while hearts is considered the middle suit or 'double menace' held by both defenders. But now supposing the defenders were able to arrange that one of them kept the double menace while the other kept the two single menaces, the declarer would be left helpless:

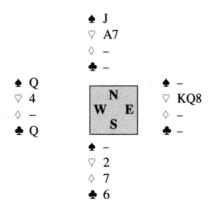

or, for that matter:

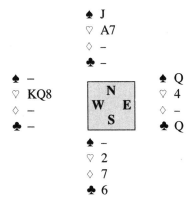

```
              ♠ J
              ♡ A7
              ◊ –
              ♣ –
  ♠ –                      ♠ Q
  ♡ KQ8     ┌─────────┐    ♡ 4
  ◊ –       │   N     │    ◊ –
  ♣ –       │ W   E   │    ♣ Q
            │   S     │
            └─────────┘
              ♠ –
              ♡ 2
              ◊ 7
              ♣ 6
```

In either case, on the lead of the winning diamond, the hand with the hearts discards the ♡8 and the hand with the black queens discards the ♡4. Declarer must concede one trick. So we can lay down our next tip:

Guiding Principle

When a double squeeze is threatened, defenders must firstly try to recognise which suits are single menaces and which is the double menace and arrange, if possible, for one of them to hold the double menace while the other holds the two singles.

Misdefences often arise when a defender holds very poor cards in a suit and fails to realise that they are not so bad after all. This is an example:

Love All. Dealer East.

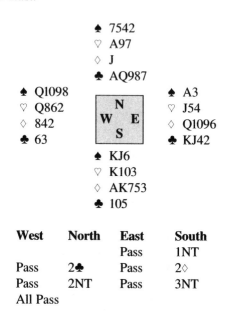

```
                    ♠ 7542
                    ♡ A97
                    ◇ J
                    ♣ AQ987
    ♠ Q1098                      ♠ A3
    ♡ Q862                       ♡ J54
    ◇ 842                        ◇ Q1096
    ♣ 63                         ♣ KJ42
                    ♠ KJ6
                    ♡ K103
                    ◇ AK753
                    ♣ 105
```

West	North	East	South
		Pass	1NT
Pass	2♣	Pass	2◇
Pass	2NT	Pass	3NT
All Pass			

North/South were playing a 13-15 point opener.

West led the ♠10, won by East who returned the suit. South's ♠J lost to West's ♠Q. Now, at this point, a diamond switch would have beaten the contract outright, but West persisted with his suit, won by South perforce as East discarded a club. Now declarer had a chance. He ran the ♣10, losing to East's ♣J and the ◇Q was returned, won by South. Another club finesse lost to East's ♣K and he now played the ◇10, won again by South while dummy discarded a low heart. Declarer now crossed to the ♡A and ran two more clubs, discarding two low diamonds from his hand while East discarded the ◇6. Keen to keep his major-suit controls intact, West discarded the ◇8 and a low heart. That completed ten tricks and this was the position just before the last winning club was cashed:

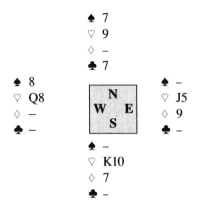

On the ♣7, East had to keep his diamond while West had to keep his spade. Both released hearts, allowing declarer the last two tricks in that suit. West was at fault in failing to follow our guiding principle above. With the double squeeze threatened, East/West had to align their defence so that one of them kept the two single menaces while the other kept the double menace. As far as the single menaces were concerned, East was out of spades; therefore it would have be West or nobody. For that reason, West had to appreciate that his ◊8 would need be high enough to control the suit, i.e. that his partner had ◊Q109 at least. On the long clubs, he discards two hearts and now the end position becomes:

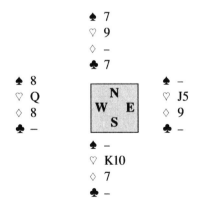

Now, on the ♣7, East can take responsibility for hearts by releasing the ◊9 and West will simply follow South's discard. On the ◊7, he throws the ◊8, protecting his partner against a heart finesse. On the ♡10, he throws the ♡Q. Either way, the defenders cannot be denied a fifth trick.

In these double-squeeze positions, both defenders are threatened. We now turn to positions were only one defender is under pressure in three suits and there is a danger of what is called a 'triple squeeze' repeating to earn declarer two extra tricks.

This is a typical matrix in which clubs are trumps or declarer has set up a long club suit at no-trumps:

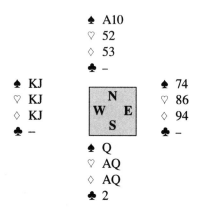

♠ A10
♡ 52
◇ 53
♣ −

♠ KJ
♡ KJ
◇ KJ
♣ −

♠ 74
♡ 86
◇ 94
♣ −

♠ Q
♡ AQ
◇ AQ
♣ 2

In this diagram, declarer, needing all six of the remaining tricks, appears to have only four on top, the long club and the three aces, but observe that West comes under terrible pressure when that winning club is played.

Suppose we try the possible discards. A diamond is no good. Declarer cashes the ◇A and ◇Q and West is in more trouble in this position:

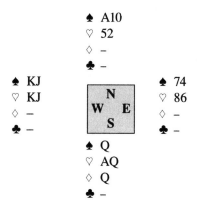

♠ A10
♡ 52
◇ −
♣ −

♠ KJ
♡ KJ
◇ −
♣ −

♠ 74
♡ 86
◇ −
♣ −

♠ Q
♡ AQ
◇ Q
♣ −

He is now squeezed in the majors. Discarding a heart is no better. Now declarer cashes the ♡A and ♡Q, similarly squeezing West in spades and diamonds.

But now try the effect of a spade discard. This admittedly gives declarer an extra trick in that suit in dummy, but now the squeeze does not repeat. On the ♠10, the position is:

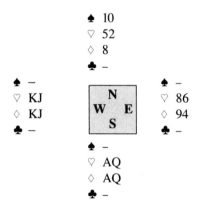

```
              ♠ 10
              ♡ 52
              ◇ 8
              ♣ -

♠ -                        ♠ -
♡ KJ        N              ♡ 86
◇ KJ      W   E            ◇ 94
♣ -         S              ♣ -

              ♠ -
              ♡ AQ
              ◇ AQ
              ♣ -
```

Now there is a light at the end of tunnel in that South has to discard ahead of West. West will simply follow South's discard and declarer will have to concede one trick. Thus, with correct defence, the squeeze has produced only one rather than two extra tricks. West had to ensure keeping the positions in the suits held by South so that he could avoid committing himself too early on the second squeeze card. We can thus lay down the rule:

Guiding Principle

When threatened in three suits, it will usually be right to abandon the suit held over you, and keep the suits held under you to avoid the squeeze repeating.

Notice that the size of the small red cards in the East and North hands are relevant and, indeed, if the North cards are higher, the defenders may be helpless anyway.

Suppose we alter the above initial diagram to this:

```
              ♠ A10
              ♡ 86
              ◇ 94
              ♣ –
   ♠ KJ                      ♠ 74
   ♡ KJ         N            ♡ 52
   ◇ KJ      W     E         ◇ 53
   ♣ –          S            ♣ –
              ♠ Q
              ♡ AQ
              ◇ AQ
              ♣ 2
```

Now even the correct defence offers no hope. On the ♣2, West discards a spade and North a heart. Now before cashing his spades, South cashes his ◇A so that now the ◇9 will act as a menace. The two spades are now cashed, but on the second South discards the ◇Q and West is helpless.

In the above example, we had one suit held over with two held under so we could follow the rule to advantage. The obvious question arises of what happens if two are held over and under. We shall a look at a position where the heart menace has moved up North, and observe now that East is out of it completely:

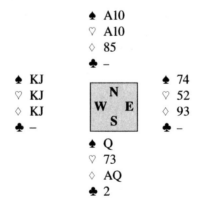

```
              ♠ A10
              ♡ A10
              ◇ 85
              ♣ –
   ♠ KJ                      ♠ 74
   ♡ KJ         N            ♡ 52
   ◇ KJ      W     E         ◇ 93
   ♣ –          S            ♣ –
              ♠ Q
              ♡ 73
              ◇ AQ
              ♣ 2
```

Now, on the ♣2, whichever suit West abandons, he will be subjected to a further squeeze when two more rounds of that suit are cashed. There is nothing to be done.

Therefore we shall concentrate on cases where the defenders have a chance and look at a full deal:

North/South Game. Dealer East.

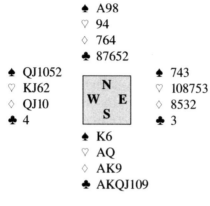

```
                    ♠ A98
                    ♡ 94
                    ◇ 764
                    ♣ 87652
    ♠ QJ1052                      ♠ 743
    ♡ KJ62         ┌─────┐        ♡ 108753
    ◇ QJ10         │  N  │        ◇ 8532
    ♣ 4            │W   E│        ♣ 3
                   │  S  │
                   └─────┘
                    ♠ K6
                    ♡ AQ
                    ◇ AK9
                    ♣ AKQJ109
```

West	North	East	South
		Pass	1♣
Dble	Pass	1♡	2♡
Pass	3♣	Pass	4NT
Pass	5◇	Pass	7♣
All Pass			

North/South were playing a strong club and West's double showed the majors. South should have devalued his major holdings, but hoped for ruffing values from his partner; sadly no joy. West led the ♠Q which declarer won in hand. He could see eleven top tricks and, with the heart finesse almost certainly wrong, his aim was to put pressure on West. He thus cashed five rounds of trumps, leaving this position after six tricks:

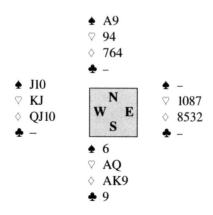

```
                    ♠ A9
                    ♡ 94
                    ◇ 764
                    ♣ -
    ♠ J10                          ♠ -
    ♡ KJ           ┌─────┐        ♡ 1087
    ◇ QJ10         │  N  │        ◇ 8532
    ♣ -            │W   E│        ♣ -
                   │  S  │
                   └─────┘
                    ♠ 6
                    ♡ AQ
                    ◇ AK9
                    ♣ 9
```

On the ♣9, West had to find a further discard. A diamond allows three rounds for South, which will squeeze West again in the majors. A heart allows two rounds of the suit, again squeezing West, this time in spades and diamonds. Only a spade gives the defence a chance. Now two rounds of spades force South to discard ahead of West. However, note the importance of the positions of the ◇7 and ◇8. Change them round and South simply cashes the ◇A and ◇K before taking his two spade tricks in this position:

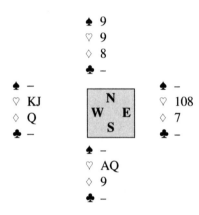

Now on the ♣9, South can spare the ◇9 and West is squeezed in the red suits, the ◇8 in dummy acting as the crucial menace.

In the light of this, we can lay down a further tip, which is very much neglected, even in top-class circles:

Guiding Principle

If you have a very poor hand and partner is clearly threatened with a squeeze, take care in keeping small cards which may be of help. Here the diamonds are a case in point. When East sees the dummy and observes that his ◇8 is higher than dummy's highest diamond, the ◇7, that is the suit to hold.

We conclude this chapter with some exercises on advanced squeeze defence. You will need to recognise which type of the two squeezes we discussed is threatened and what action to take.

Quiz on advanced squeeze defence

Problem 7.6
North/South Game. Dealer West.

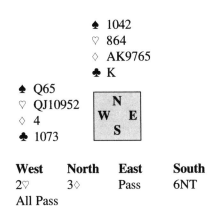

```
              ♠ 1042
              ♡ 864
              ◊ AK9765
              ♣ K
  ♠ Q65      ┌─────┐
  ♡ QJ10952  │  N  │
  ◊ 4        │W   E│
  ♣ 1073     │  S  │
             └─────┘
```

West	North	East	South
2♡	3◊	Pass	6NT
All Pass			

North was obviously unhappy to be preempted out of the auction.

You lead the ♡Q to partner's ♡A and he returns the ♡3 to declarer's ♡K. Declarer crosses the ♣K, partner following with the ♣6, and returns to hand with the ◊Q, partner following with the ◊2. He now cashes the ♣A, partner following the ♣4 while dummy discards a low spade. Now comes the ◊J, on which partner plays the ◊3, and the rest of the diamond suit follows. How do you plan your defence?

Problem 7.7
Game All. Dealer West.

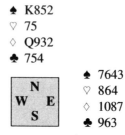

♠ K852
♡ 75
◇ Q932
♣ 754

♠ 7643
♡ 864
◇ 1087
♣ 963

West	North	East	South
1♡	Pass	Pass	2♡
Pass	2♠	Pass	3◇
Pass	5◇	Pass	6◇
All Pass			

South's 2♡ was played as a very strong hand, forcing at least to suit agreement or game.

Partner leads the ♣K, which is allowed to hold, South playing the ♣2. On the ♠Q, South wins with the ♠A in hand and cashes the ◇A, partner discarding the ♡J. On the assumption that more diamonds are coming, how do you plan the defence?

Problem 7.8
North/South Game. Dealer East.

♠ A72
♡ A10942
◇ A6
♣ K42

♠ 985
♡ Q876
◇ 10987
♣ 96

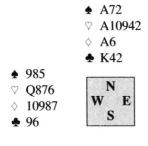

West	North	East	South
		Pass	1◇
Pass	1♡	Pass	3♣
Pass	3♠	Pass	3NT
Pass	7NT	All Pass	

Trailing badly in a teams match, North decided to take a shot at a grand slam.

Deciding that the ◇10 was the lead least likely to give anything away, you lead that card and note that North has, to say the least of it, pushed the boat out. Dummy's ◇A wins as partner follows with the ◇4. A low heart to the ♡K follows, partner playing the ♡3 and then a club to dummy's ♣K, partner playing the ♣7. The ♡A is cashed, partner playing the ♡5 while declarer discards the ♠3. Now follows a club to the ♣A, partner playing the ♣8, and then the ♣Q. What do you discard?

Problem 7.9
North/South Game. Dealer South.

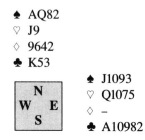

♠ AQ82
♡ J9
◊ 9642
♣ K53

                    ♠ J1093
                    ♡ Q1075
                    ◊ –
                    ♣ A10982

West	North	East	South
			1NT
Pass	2♣	Dble	2◊
Pass	3NT	All Pass	

South showed 15-17 points and a Stayman sequence followed.

Partner dutifully leads the ♣Q, which holds, as does the ♣J, South following with the ♣4 and ♣6. West switches to the ♠7, won by dummy's ♠A, South following with the ♠4. Dummy's ◊9 is run to partner's ◊J and you can easily afford a heart discard. West plays a second spade, won by South's ♠K. South's ◊Q is won by West's ◊K and he returns the ◊3 indicating that he started with five diamonds; you discard another club as South wins. South now cashes a fourth round of diamonds and you can see:

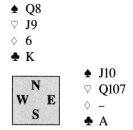

♠ Q8
♡ J9
◊ 6
♣ K

                    ♠ J10
                    ♡ Q107
                    ◊ –
                    ♣ A

West and dummy are still following, but what do you discard?

Solutions

Problem 7.6

In spite of the bidding, prospects look distinctly grim. Declarer looks set for six diamond tricks, two top clubs and the ♡K already taken to total nine so far. He will almost certainly need the two top spades to justify his bidding which makes eleven, implying that partner will have to hold the ♣Q. The crucial question now is the whereabouts of the two black jacks. On completion of the diamonds, you will be down to three cards. Clearly you will have to hold one top heart and therefore at most two spades, implying the need for partner to have the ♠J or declarer to misguess. How about partner? He will need to hold a club guard and therefore at most two spades. It is no good. So you must think again. A double squeeze is threatened and you must observe the rule of one defender keeping two single menaces while the other holds the middle suit. The single menaces are hearts and clubs and, if you are to hold clubs effectively, you will have to credit partner with the ♣J. (Incidentally, with one trick in the bag, partner might have made life easier for you by dropping the ♣Q on the first round, but few defend so well.) So having placed every card, this will be the deal:

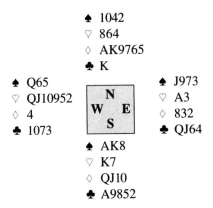

		♠ 1042		
		♡ 864		
		◇ AK9765		
		♣ K		

♠ Q65				♠ J973
♡ QJ10952		N		♡ A3
◇ 4	W		E	◇ 832
♣ 1073		S		♣ QJ64

		♠ AK8		
		♡ K7		
		◇ QJ10		
		♣ A9852		

You must be the one to guard clubs by hanging on to your ♣10 and coming down to the ♠Q, ♡J and ♣10 while partner keeps ♠J97 and throws his club honours.

Of course 6◇ would have been easier as a long club can be ruffed high, but on that auction South understandably wanted to be declarer.

Problem 7.7

Counting tricks, you see that declarer has one club, six diamonds and two spades to total nine so far and partner's failure to touch hearts indicates a probable ♡AQ doubleton with South to take his total to ten. Two further tricks will be needed and all the indications are that declarer will angle for a progressive triple squeeze against West. The question is: "Can you help?" In situations like this, it is very easy to lose interest. You can easily spare a heart on the fourth diamond, but then you will be able to see this:

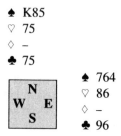

```
            ♠ K85
            ♡ 75
            ◇ -
            ♣ 75
                        ♠ 764
              N         ♡ 86
            W   E       ◇ -
              S         ♣ 96
```

On the fifth round, what will you discard? The crucial point is that you must keep parity with dummy, following suit. Partner will have to observe the rule of abandoning the suit on his left, namely spades, but that will not be until the sixth trump. Meanwhile, you are under pressure now. Suppose dummy discards a club. If you discard a spade, the whole spade suit comes in and declarer makes six diamond tricks, four spades and the other two aces. If you discard a heart, South cashes his last diamond, on which partner abandons spades, and then the ♡A, after which he takes his two spade tricks, the second in this position:

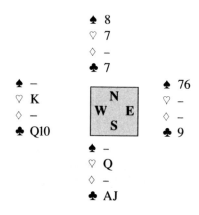

```
              ♠ 8
              ♡ 7
              ◇ -
              ♣ 7
    ♠ -                     ♠ 76
    ♡ K         N           ♡ -
    ◇ -       W   E         ◇ -
    ♣ Q10       S           ♣ 9
              ♠ -
              ♡ Q
              ◇ -
              ♣ AJ
```

The ♡Q is discarded on the ♠8 and West is finished because you promoted the ♡7. As long as you discard a club, your partner cannot be hurt. Similar arguments apply if dummy discards a heart and you fail to follow. Again, a spade discard allows the whole suit to come in, while a club allows South to cash his ♣A and then take his two spades, discarding his ♣J on the second. Dummy's ♣7 becomes the crucial menace. Finally, if dummy discards a spade, you must keep both your heart and club holdings intact to avoid a menace in either suit being promoted in dummy:

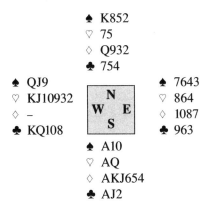

```
              ♠ K852
              ♡ 75
              ◊ Q932
              ♣ 754
♠ QJ9                      ♠ 7643
♡ KJ10932      N          ♡ 864
◊ –         W     E       ◊ 1087
♣ KQ108        S          ♣ 963
              ♠ A10
              ♡ AQ
              ◊ AKJ654
              ♣ AJ2
```

As long a you keep parity, you have an answer to anything declarer tries. It will be noticed that, as the cards lie, declarer could have played three rounds of spades early to establish the ♠8, but that does him no good. It sets up an eleventh trick, but that will be the last he sees of dummy and he has no hope of avoiding a loser in clubs or hearts. His line of play was the best, and only accurate defence by both East and West could beat the slam.

Problem 7.8

Despite the bidding, this looks distinctly grim. If South has both minor suits running, he will make his contract in some comfort with at least five diamonds, four clubs and two top cards in each major. If partner has the ◊J so that declarer has only three diamond tricks, he will need four club tricks on top. Then, even if the spades are good for three tricks, that will only total twelve, with no hope of a thirteenth. The critical case thus arises when South has five diamond tricks and only three club tricks to go with four tops in the majors for twelve so far. Now there is prospectively serious trouble. East is in sole charge of the clubs and if you decide to hold the heart position, you will put the partnership in a classic double-squeeze alignment in that neither of you will be able to hold the spades.

You have to obey the rule that one partner must hold the two single menaces, here clubs and hearts, and the other the middle suit; spades. Only partner can hold the club and thus he must hold the heart and you the spade which implies that your ♠9 must come into the reckoning, i.e. that partner holds ♠QJ10; there is no other hope:

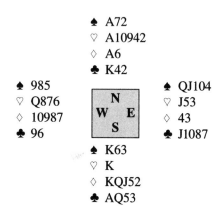

```
                    ♠ A72
                    ♡ A10942
                    ◇ A6
                    ♣ K42
    ♠ 985                          ♠ QJ104
    ♡ Q876          N              ♡ J53
    ◇ 10987       W   E            ◇ 43
    ♣ 96            S              ♣ J1087
                    ♠ K63
                    ♡ K
                    ◇ KQJ52
                    ♣ AQ53
```

For that reason, you must hold all three of your spades and discard hearts, now or on the run of the diamonds. If you discard a spade, partner will have to hold both black suits and leave you in charge of hearts. This will be the position just before the last diamond:

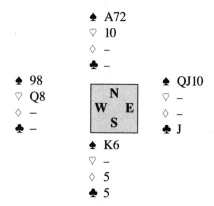

```
                    ♠ A72
                    ♡ 10
                    ◇ –
                    ♣ –
    ♠ 98                           ♠ QJ10
    ♡ Q8            N              ♡ –
    ◇ –           W   E            ◇ –
    ♣ –             S              ♣ J
                    ♠ K6
                    ♡ –
                    ◇ 5
                    ♣ 5
```

On the last diamond, you can play as you wish, but dummy discards the ♡10 and East is squeezed in the black suits. If you hold the spades, it will look like this:

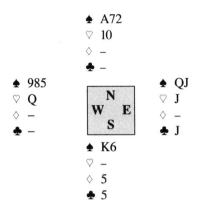

♠ A72
♡ 10
◇ –
♣ –

♠ 985　　　　　　　　♠ QJ
♡ Q　　　　　　　　　♡ J
◇ –　　　　　　　　　◇ –
♣ –　　　　　　　　　♣ J

♠ K6
♡ –
◇ 5
♣ 5

Now you can discard your ♡Q on the last diamond and East can hold his club and heart – no problem.

Problem 7.9

All the points that your partner can have are now accounted for. You are clearly squeezed in three suits and must try not to give *two* tricks away by following the rule of discarding the suit held to your left, namely hearts. This will allow South to cash three hearts, but, on the third round, dummy will have to discard ahead of you and the defence cannot be denied a fifth trick:

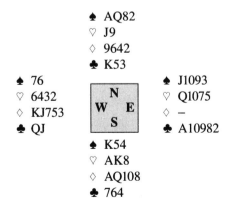

♠ AQ82
♡ J9
◇ 9642
♣ K53

♠ 76　　　　　　　　♠ J1093
♡ 6432　　　　　　　♡ Q1075
◇ KJ753　　　　　　　◇ –
♣ QJ　　　　　　　　♣ A10982

♠ K54
♡ AK8
◇ AQ108
♣ 764

Satisfy yourself again that, if you discard the ♣A, the ♣K will squeeze you again in the majors and that, if you discard a spade, two rounds of spades from dummy will squeeze you in clubs and hearts. Note that, if West has the ♡8 and South a lower card, the contract goes down two tricks.

Chapter 8

The Other Point of View

Up to now, we have concentrated on defenders' discards. However, despite the very considerable volume of bridge literature, little or nothing has been written on the subject of discarding by declarer from his own hand and from dummy. Few defenders appreciate that this again is a largely untapped mine of information. The observant defender will save himself a lot of mistakes if he uses that information to place unseen cards.

Consider this example where you are West:

North/South Game. Dealer South.

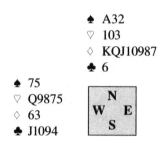

```
                        ♠ A32
                        ♡ 103
                        ◊ KQJ10987
                        ♣ 6
        ♠ 75
        ♡ Q9875         N
        ◊ 63          W   E
        ♣ J1094          S
```

West	North	East	South
			1♡
Pass	2◊	Pass	2♠
Pass	3◊	Pass	3NT
All Pass			

After a two-over one bid by North, South's reverse was game-forcing.

You lead the ♣J to partner's ♣A and he returns the ♣5 to South's ♣K. You are already resigned to having to sit through a long string of diamonds, but then the incredible happens. Dummy discards a diamond! What does that tell you? With a certain entry to dummy, declarer only needs a small singleton diamond to be able to knock out the ◊A and then enjoy the rest of the suit. When he discards a diamond, that is ruled out. The only explanation is that he is 4504 and cannot use the suit. You can now place partner with 4144 and plan your defence accordingly.

Having seen the idea, what would you make of this, again sitting West?

Love All. Dealer East.

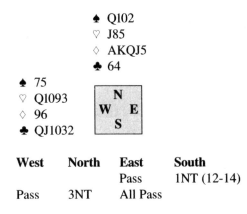

```
                 ♠ Q102
                 ♡ J85
                 ◊ AKQJ5
                 ♣ 64
    ♠ 75        ┌──────────┐
    ♡ Q1093     │    N     │
    ◊ 96        │  W    E  │
    ♣ QJ1032    │    S     │
                └──────────┘
```

West	North	East	South
		Pass	1NT (12-14)
Pass	3NT	All Pass	

You lead the ♣Q, won by partner's ♣A. He returns the ♣9, which is allowed to hold. On the third round, South's ♣K wins and again the incredible happens. Dummy discards the ◊J. There is only one explanation. South would not deliberately throw a diamond trick away like this; why should he? The answer is: he hasn't! He has five diamonds in his own hand and wants to keep his options open in the major suits as long as possible as well as keeping maximum fluidity with entries in the diamond suit. It is amazing what you can find out if only, as one of my students once put it, you creep into his mind. Here you can thus place him with 3253 or 2353 with confidence.

So we can lay down the relevant tip in this area:

Guiding Principle

If declarer makes a discard for his own hand or dummy, assume that he does not need that card and insist on knowing, in your own mind, why! As we have already seen, possible explanations include:

a) discarding a loser, or
b) discarding a winner which he cannot reach or
c) discarding from a suit in which he has sufficient winners in the other hand.

Now try the following examples, using the information from declarer's discards to place the unseen cards and plan your defence.

Quiz on declarer discards

Problem 8.1
Love All. Dealer North.

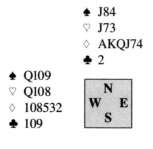

                    ♠ J84
                    ♡ J73
                    ◇ AKQJ74
                    ♣ 2
        ♠ Q109
        ♡ Q108   N
        ◇ 108532   W   E
        ♣ 109   S

West	North	East	South
	1◇	Pass	4NT
Pass	5◇	Pass	7NT
All Pass			

You lead the ♣10 and South's ♣A wins, East following with the ♣3. On the ♣K, dummy discards a low diamond, as East follows with the ♣4. What do you discard on the ♣Q? Would it make any difference if dummy discards a low heart or a low spade?

Problem 8.2
Game All. Dealer East.

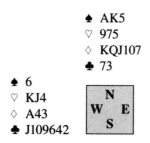

                    ♠ AK5
                    ♡ 975
                    ◇ KQJ107
                    ♣ 73
        ♠ 6
        ♡ KJ4   N
        ◇ A43   W   E
        ♣ J109642   S

West	North	East	South
		Pass	1♠
Pass	2◊	Pass	2♡
Pass	4♠	All Pass	

You lead the ♣J to the ♣3, ♣K and ♣A. All follow to the ♠Q and you discard the ♣6 on the second round of trumps to dummy. Now declarer calls for the ◊K; partner plays the ◊9 and South discards the ♡2. How do you defend?

Problem 8.3
East/West Game. Dealer North.

```
                    ♠ KQJ1093
                    ♡ 74
                    ◊ AQ2
                    ♣ 72
      ♠ A8754       ┌─────────┐
      ♡ K983        │    N    │
      ◊ 5           │  W   E  │
      ♣ K106        │    S    │
                    └─────────┘
```

West	North	East	South
	1♠	Pass	2◊
Pass	2♠	Pass	3♡
Pass	4◊	Pass	6◊
All Pass			

You lead your trump and dummy's ◊Q wins, East playing the ◊3 and South the ◊4. Declarer calls for the ♠K to East's ♠6 and South discards the ♡2. How do you defend?

Problem 8.4
East/West Game. Dealer South.

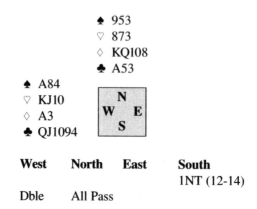

♠ 953
♡ 873
◇ KQ108
♣ A53

♠ A84
♡ KJ10
◇ A3
♣ QJ1094

West	North	East	South
			1NT (12-14)
Dble	All Pass		

You lead the ♣Q and it holds, dummy playing the ♣3, East the ♣2 and South the ♣6. On the second round, dummy plays low again, partner the ♣8 and South wins with the ♣K. South's ◇9 holds and you have to win the second round, partner playing the ◇2 and ◇7. Your ♣J forces dummy's ♣A, partner following with the ♣7 while declarer discards the ♠2. Declarer cashes two more diamonds, following himself while partner follows with the ◇5 and then discards the ♡5 and you the ♡10 and ♣4. Now a spade runs to South's ♠J and your ♠A and you cash the last two clubs, partner discarding two more low hearts and declarer the ♡9 and ♠7. How do you continue?

Problem 8.5
East/West Game. Dealer South.

♠ 953
♡ 873
◇ KQ108
♣ A53

♠ QJ72
♡ AQ9
◇ J964
♣ K6

West	North	East	South
			1NT
Dble	All Pass		

You allow West's ♣Q to hold and win the second round with ♣K. You attack diamonds and West wins the second round before persisting with clubs. You take dummy's ♣A. What do you play next?

Solutions

Problem 8.1

This is horrible and the first rule here is to keep your head. What has South got for this bid without any investigation at all? Almost certainly a tremendous club suit and the major aces and at least one of the major kings if not both as well. Note that he did not ask for kings. So you must count his tricks: probably six or seven clubs and the two aces to make eight or nine so far which means it is almost certain, that if those diamonds come in for four tricks, never mind the long cards, the contract will be made. The critical case arises where South is void of diamonds in this kind of layout:

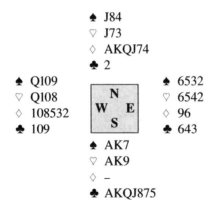

```
              ♠ J84
              ♡ J73
              ◇ AKQJ74
              ♣ 2
  ♠ Q109                  ♠ 6532
  ♡ Q108      N           ♡ 6542
  ◇ 108532  W   E         ◇ 96
  ♣ 109       S           ♣ 643
              ♠ AK7
              ♡ AK9
              ◇ -
              ♣ AKQJ875
```

Now you must protect your two queens like grim death and discard diamonds. If dummy discards from one of his major-suit holdings, it makes no difference. Remember you will have to find four or five discards and thus keeping diamonds implies that you will have to abandon both your queens – unlikely to be right. Obviously here declarer is correct to discard low diamonds early as a major-suit queen may be dropping doubleton.

Problem 8.2

You should have noticed a number of important points. Firstly, South still has the ♣Q and there is no future in that suit. Secondly, partner played the ◇9 from a holding of five cards. Count is not relevant here. It should be obvious to both defenders that South is void of diamonds. Otherwise, he could have played the suit from his hand at an early stage, possibly putting West to an awkward decision before East could indicate count. Thirdly, if the defenders are going to have any joy, it will be in hearts and the suit must be attacked immediately. What is this about not leading away from KJx, least of all round to a bid suit? Here it is the only hope and you must win the diamond immediately (there is nothing to be gained by ducking and to do so would amount to missing the boat) and switch to your low heart. The deal:

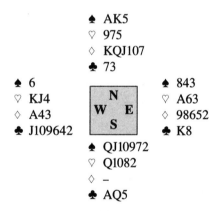

```
                  ♠ AK5
                  ♡ 975
                  ◇ KQJ107
                  ♣ 73
  ♠ 6                          ♠ 843
  ♡ KJ4          N             ♡ A63
  ◇ A43      W       E         ◇ 98652
  ♣ J109642      S             ♣ K8
                  ♠ QJ10972
                  ♡ Q1082
                  ◇ –
                  ♣ AQ5
```

Note that even if your heart lead *is* into a tenace, it costs nothing. Any losers in the South hand were going away on the diamonds anyway.

This is very often the case when a defender is faced with leading away from such a holding and a tip is in order here.

Guiding Principle

If you are hesitant to lead away from an unpleasant tenace holding because you fear it will cost a trick (not to mention involving your listening to a beginners' lecture from partner) ask yourself if declarer's losers are going away anyway. If they are, there is nothing to lose and you should not stand on ceremony; your position in the post-mortem is perfectly safe.

Problem 8.3

This seems remarkably similar to the last problem, but how appearances can be deceptive! You should realise that, with potential winners in both clubs and hearts in your hand, the whole spade suit, (four tricks at least, anyway) will have to brought in if declarer is to succeed. Furthermore, South will have to have both ♣A and ♡A if his bidding makes any sense and this is therefore not a situation where you can win the spade now and cash out. In fact, if you do, declarer will be able to clear trumps, ending in dummy, and make the contract. Your thoughts must consequently be directed to stopping the run of the spades. You must refuse two rounds, allowing partner to step in with a trump on the third. Declarer can overruff, but your ♠A remains intact and the rest of the spades are now valueless. Declarer will be able to arrange for a ruff in dummy, but will lose at least two tricks. The deal:

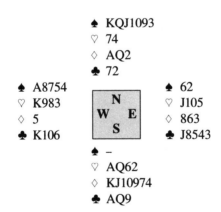

```
                        ♠ KQJ1093
                        ♡ 74
                        ◊ AQ2
                        ♣ 72
        ♠ A8754                         ♠ 62
        ♡ K983          N               ♡ J105
        ◊ 5           W   E             ◊ 863
        ♣ K106          S               ♣ J8543
                        ♠ –
                        ♡ AQ62
                        ◊ KJ10974
                        ♣ AQ9
```

Note that it is not good enough to win the second spade and return the suit for partner to ruff. South overruffs, draws trumps, ending in dummy and cashes enough spades to discard his losers. Six diamonds, four spades and two other aces add up to twelve.

Problem 8.4

This is very simple. Partner has twice indicated a spade holding and you have forced South down to the ♠Q and ♡AQ. You can now lead your remaining spade for partner to cash two more spades to defeat the hand. We shall look at the deal in a moment.

Problem 8.5

This is the same problem as 8.4 as viewed by declarer. The critical point comes after the ♣A has being knocked out. If you cash your diamond winners now, you will have tightened the position against yourself and, after losing a spade trick, will have no convenient discard on the last club. However, if you play spades immediately, you can discard a diamond on the last club, keeping communication with dummy and now the tables are turned on the defenders as West as no answer. The deal:

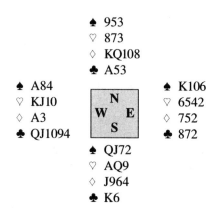

```
              ♠ 953
              ♡ 873
              ◊ KQ108
              ♣ A53
♠ A84      ┌─────────┐   ♠ K106
♡ KJ10     │    N    │   ♡ 6542
◊ A3       │  W   E  │   ◊ 752
♣ QJ1094   │    S    │   ♣ 872
           └─────────┘
              ♠ QJ72
              ♡ AQ9
              ◊ J964
              ♣ K6
```

We shall play the hand both ways and watch what happens. In both problems, we started with two rounds of clubs then two rounds of diamonds and a third club to dummy's ♣A, leaving:

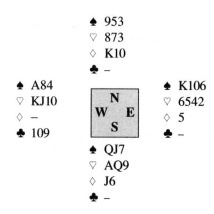

```
              ♠ 953
              ♡ 873
              ◊ K10
              ♣ -
♠ A84      ┌─────────┐   ♠ K106
♡ KJ10     │    N    │   ♡ 6542
◊ -        │  W   E  │   ◊ 5
♣ 109      │    S    │   ♣ -
           └─────────┘
              ♠ QJ7
              ♡ AQ9
              ◊ J6
              ♣ -
```

Now, if declarer cashes his diamonds and then plays a spade, West will win and cash his clubs; on the last one, we have:

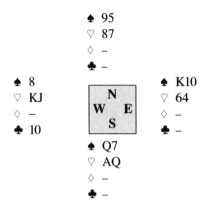

    ♠ 95
    ♡ 87
    ◊ –
    ♣ –

♠ 8   ♠ K10
♡ KJ   ♡ 64
◊ –   ◊ –
♣ 10   ♣ –

    ♠ Q7
    ♡ AQ
    ◊ –
    ♣ –

On the last club, South is stuck. If he discards his ♡Q, West plays hearts and the defenders take the last two tricks. If he blanks his ♠Q, as he did in the problem, defenders cash their two spades immediately.

But now we shall replay the hand the correct way, where declarer played spades before cashing his diamonds. Again, West wins and cashes two clubs, but South can throw a diamond; we are now down to:

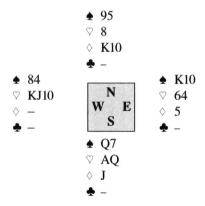

    ♠ 95
    ♡ 8
    ◊ K10
    ♣ –

♠ 84   ♠ K10
♡ KJ10   ♡ 64
◊ –   ◊ 5
♣ –   ♣ –

    ♠ Q7
    ♡ AQ
    ◊ J
    ♣ –

and whatever West plays now, South cannot be denied four more tricks and the contract. By cashing his diamonds too early, South effectively tightened the position against himself, what is known in squeeze jargon as 'rectifying the count'.

This kind of position occurs frequently, notably in low level no-trump contracts of which 1NT doubled is probably the most frequent.

It shows how watchful you have to be on everybody's carding and discarding which is the principal message of this book from which I hope you have derived worthwhile benefit.